Living Gratitude

A Simple Path to Happiness

Matt O'Grady

Foreword by Jeannette Maw

Harmonia Media / New York

HarmoniaMedia.com
Huntington, NY

DISCLAIMER

This publication contains the ideas and opinions of its author. The intention of this book is to provide informative and helpful content on the subjects addressed in the publication. It is shared and sold with the understanding that the author and the publisher are not engaged in giving medical, health, or any other type of personal professional services in the book. The reader should always consult his or her medical, health, or other professional and accredited health provider before adopting any of the suggestions in this book or drawing any ideas, inferences, or practices from this book.

The author and the publisher specifically disclaim all responsibility for any liability, loss, risk, personal or otherwise which may occur as a consequence, indirectly, or directly, of the application or use of any information, content, etc. from this book.

Cover Design by Melodye Hunter

Manufactured in the United States of America

First Printing, 2015

ISBN 978-1-943672-00-4

www.mattogradycoaching.com

I dedicate this book to my greatest teachers, my
Mom and Dad, and my wife and my son.
Thank you. I love you.

Contents

Acknowledgements

A book about gratitude and appreciation should have a cool acknowledgements section, right? Well, it sure does not do you all justice, but I hope you all get a sense of my gratitude to you based on the whole book, rather than the few short notes here. Truth is, without all of you, this book would have never happened. Without all of you, I never would have loved as deeply, been as grateful, or been inspired enough to write this book. So, yes, thank you.

To my parents, thanks for giving me, well, everything! Like life, for example. Thank you for always being there with love, generosity, kindness and safety. Your patience and forgiveness taught me great lessons. Your confidence in me, your guiding lessons early on, have served me well, and because of you, I hope to help others who were not blessed with parents like you. Your consistency in reminding me how important it is to be thankful for the gifts we receive resonates deeply in this book.

To Tara, my beautiful, loving, supportive, "most fun person I've ever met" wife. You know the deal, you saved me then twenty years ago, and you save me every day. I am eternally grateful for all you have given me, and especially for believing in me.

To the best gift you ever gave me, Patrick, you are simply the best thing in my life. You took a pretty good life and have made it an extremely joyful experience I had no idea was possible until you blessed us almost four years ago.

To my dear brother, Kevin, your reliability and consistency is rivaled only by our awesome parents. Your forgiveness and acceptance of me when I wasn't a good big brother—or even a good friend—is appreciated in ways I can't go into here. Thank you. Having you and your sweet, beautiful family close by has been a great blessing to us all.

To my three big cousins, Chris, Tim and Paul, thanks for always looking out for me. I have been looking up to you as the three big brothers I never had my whole life, and you were all my first best friends. Some of your kind words, invitations and outreaches from you and your families have come at the most perfect times, when I have needed you most, even though you didn't know it.

To all my nieces, nephews and little cousins, watching you all grow up to be the smart, beautiful, impressive young men and women that you are has been one of the great joys of my life. You have all helped me open a heart that was stubborn, but I could not resist the power of you all! Thank you.

To dearly departed Aunt Rose and Aunt Judy, you both were so damn good to me, caring sweet loving whispers in my ears while being hugged at a very young age, stayed with me when I was down, and I can still hear them now. "It's OK, Matt, you are alright, I love you." Grateful.

My oldest friend, Lynnie Keating, did you get a doctorate in Friendship? You are that good at it. You have been there for almost 40 years, let's do 50 more. You are the best listener I've ever experienced! You are by far one of the most generous and thoughtful people I have ever met. Thank you for your kindness, patience, and all around great friendship for all these decades, it is greatly appreciated.

Kirsten Carle, we were instant friends. We were best friends a minute later, and we've never stopped going deep since. Your help in life on every level has been a core foundation since I've met you. Knowing and learning from you has made me a better person. Pretty much every important endeavor I've been involved with has your fingerprints of support all over it. Canvas, Harmonia Media, this book, and so much more. You are simply the best. Thank you.

Frank and Betty Crocitto, I will never forget that fateful evening I met you at the "Rumi with Classical Piano Event". My life was never the same. You opened me up to a world of Presence, Consciousness, Being, Gratitude, and so much more. You have taught me thousands of important things at the Discovery Institute and I pray to help others even in the smallest of ways you helped me. Thank God, thank you and thank Rumi! I am eternally grateful.

Norm, Tish and Pangea Farm, over the last 12-plus years, you have served as my spiritual home. Always there, always helpful, always kind, always present, always authentic. The teachings, retreats, laughs and delicious meals will always be remembered. Thank you for continuing to foster my spiritual and emotional development, as well as my meditation practice.

Annie Serrante, your kindness when I was sad and lonely was one of the best surprise blessings, I've ever had. It seeded one of the greatest friendships of my life. Your skill of deep listening and compassionate feedback opened me up to a new world of emotional intelligence, communication and self-love. Thank you.

Jack Corwin and Mary Prentice, you are the core of my CA family. Your thoughtful friendship and sweet fun-filled philosophy has been a pleasure to emulate! Thank you.

Dona Ho Lightsey, thank you being such an amazing friend, spiritual guide and for introducing me to some deep spiritual healing and the power of the Goddess!

Jennifer Urezzio, thank you for my Soul Languages, for being a great friend and teacher during such a tough transition in my life when I was truly embracing my spirituality for the first time.

Jason Stern, you were a great teacher, spiritual friend and housemate at times when I really needed it. You were a generous boss and a great business mentor. Thank you.

Valerie Stephenson, especially when I really needed it, your presence, kindness, friendship and belief in me was extremely helpful. Your lesson that, 'If people could be doing better, they would be', has helped me develop much more patience and compassion for others than I had before I met you. Thank you.

Phil Giuliano, thanks for being such a true friend, believing in me—and us—to create such an amazing radio show that is closing in on 200,000 downloads in 5 years. Wow. Super Grateful.

Jeannette Maw, thank you for an amazing foreword! Your community, GoodVibeU.com, has been the most spectacular community of Deliberate Creators. Thank you for all you have done, shared and given. You are one of kind, and I hope to work with even more in the future. I appreciate you.

Greg Kuhn, thanks for the epic testimonial on the back cover! Your friendship, guidance and support are bar-none. You are one cool quantum physicist!

Bill King, thanks for being an inspiring friend. You really helped me move this book forward. I am thankful to you.

Liz Sumner, your support has been tremendously consistent. Harmonia Media, this book, my coaching business, would not be anywhere near where it is without your expert help. This is just the beginning! Thank you.

Bhavini Mehta, I've only known you a short time relative to most people here, but you have proven yourself time and again. You are one of my most trusted and passionate team members. Thank you.

Holly Hunt, I am so glad to have finally found my long-term editor. You are a great editor and I appreciate all your efforts. I hope you are ready to do three more books this upcoming year!

All my friends, co-workers, clients, and just all around awesome peeps that I could not mention here, I will get you in the next book, trust me. Just because your name isn't listed here, doesn't mean I am not grateful. Thank you. I love you.

To those who didn't believe in me, thank you all the more. Your lack of confidence in me steeled my soul. Your doubt strengthened my reserve. We all have a part to play in one another's lives, and your part for me was to help me grow, stretch and find my own belief in myself. I cannot thank you enough.

Foreword

Some things can be faked. Rolex watches, identity cards and orgasms, sure, but appreciation isn't one of them. Appreciation is the ticket to a happy life. Not fame and fortune, success or material rewards—even with those things, if we aren't grateful for the life we're living, none of the traditional trappings of success will make up for it.

Being thankful for the blessings we experience, no matter what form they take in our personal situation, is absolutely required for us to experience lasting happiness. That doesn't mean, however, that some of us won't try to fake appreciation. Whether we think we should feel grateful because of social expectations, or because we're not comfortable with less gracious emotions, or even because we know the power of dialing in on this vibration, sometimes we find ourselves trying to conjure up a feeling that isn't really there.

We've all experienced it before: the cashier who half-heartedly mumbles, "Thank you for coming in." The friend who gushes appreciatively but carefully pockets the gift receipt. The co-worker who responds to sound advice with, "Thanks for your suggestion, but..." Sometimes it's us, faking gratitude to make ourselves to feel better. "At least I have my health," or, "If nothing else, this failure has taught me a valuable lesson."

But pretending to feel gratitude doesn't fly. This is why it's so important to learn the power of appreciation, as well as the skills to feel it in genuine form. One of the many reasons I am so pleased to write this foreword for Matt O'Grady is that he is a guy who exudes thankfulness in abundance, and doesn't fake it.

There have been several occasions when I've been impressed with his genuine ability to feel and express gratitude, when all I can come up with is irritation or four-letter words! This guy walks the talk, and he didn't get that way by accident. It's not that Matt was born into an exceptionally easy life, or lucked upon a gratitude gene the rest of us seem to be missing. He learned the power and skill of appreciation by purposely practicing it, and he does it so well!

You and I are fortunate enough to be able to learn from his outstanding example of why and how to introduce more appreciation into our own emotional skill sets. I personally experienced the power of appreciation after finding myself in the midst of an extremely challenging relationship with a new neighbor. Drug dealing, death threats, police raids, were the norm at his house and I was headed in a downward spiral of resistance living next door to this.

Eventually, I realized that battling the situation wouldn't fix it. What I needed to do was stop fighting and start moving toward peace and love. I began that process by looking for things to appreciate. My neighbor was industrious, operating on very little sleep. He seemed to be doing pretty good business. He had the cops figured out! He knew exactly how to handle their interference. Even I had to admit he was pretty clever, for a crackhead.

It was a struggle at first, but I knew that this was my only hope for feeling better. Relying on him to change so I could find peace and happiness was not a good bet! That's a sucker's game, depending on external circumstances to determine how we feel. Deliberate creators know better.

So I practiced thoughts of love and appreciation for my neighbor, and within several weeks (it took a while to get the hang of it!), our relationship had transformed. In fact, just today, I was in my old neighborhood and I hoped I would get a chance to visit with my old neighbor. He had become sensitive, compassionate, considerate, helpful, all the things I was certain he could never be—all because I purposely practiced appreciation. It is that magical.

I've heard stories of people who transformed their lives simply by engaging in the habit of writing down three things they're thankful for each day. I've seen bodies heal when resentments are given up in favor of appreciation. I've personally experienced nasty breakups turn into deeper love by engaging the power of looking at what there is to be thankful for.

I don't believe there's a more powerful skill for any person, let alone a deliberate creator, to engage. And you could not be in better hands to learn this skill than with Matt O'Grady.

Namaste,
Jeannette Maw
TheGoodVibeCoach.com
GoodVibeU.com

Living Gratitude

Introduction

"Gratitude unlocks the fullness of life. It turns what we have into enough, and more. It turns denial into acceptance, chaos to order, confusion to clarity. It can turn a meal into a feast, a house into a home, a stranger into a friend."

--Melody Beattie

There have been several periods in my life during which I lived in a world of darkness. Times when I felt generally irritated, frustrated and angry, and therefore sought out the short-term pleasure of primal desires: food, competition and/or sex. But the respite was short-lived, and sometimes I felt worse afterwards than I had before. At times, my body was so pain-racked and my mental state was one of such depression and sadness that I didn't feel I could share it with anyone. I thought it would take a miracle to turn my life around. It did, and it didn't.

Miraculously, I discovered a practice that saved me. Even more miraculous was the fact that it didn't take years of study in an ashram. It didn't require a thousand hours of meditation. It didn't rely on a particular religion, faith or teaching. There was no indoctrination, no membership requirement and no training manual. Before I describe the miracle, let me paint a picture of my life at the time, so you can understand that I'm not any different from you. I didn't have any special circumstances that made me better or more ready for a miracle than anyone else.

In the Navy at 24 years old, I was living what I considered to be the Life of Riley. I had already attained my degree in psychology and sociology from Hofstra University, but I wasn't interested in going down the conventional path, instead, I chose a life of partying and having a good time.

I was bartending in nightclubs on Long Island and in NYC, making a few thousand dollars in cash just about every week, slinging drinks at The Limelight, The Tunnel, Palladium, and several other iconic New York bars that were like the Studio 54 of the 1990s. Parties could last two or three days at a time, and I felt like I was on a constant adrenaline high.

But the longer I stayed in the scene, the more I began to notice things I didn't like; situations around me, my friends, co-workers and even young girls at the bar, were often treated in ways that made me uncomfortable, and I wasn't in a position to do anything about it. I saw people getting into trouble, getting sick, developing addictions that they couldn't shake. A couple of people I knew even died. I felt like I needed to slow down, and when I witnessed a gun being pulled out one night during a fight while working at a club, I knew I needed to put the brakes on my lifestyle. I asked myself, "Is this really where I want to be?"

It had been an exciting time, and I managed to make and save a lot of money, but I had been doing this since I was 19, and I realized I was tired of it all. I wanted to do something different, something meaningful. I wanted to shake up my life, leave all the crazy partying behind. I needed to get to know myself and do something good for the world. I also wanted to challenge myself, physically, mentally and emotionally.

I narrowed my options down to pursuing a graduate degree in cognitive psychology, signing up for the Peace Corps, or joining the Navy to become a Navy Seal. I know those are wildly divergent paths, and a pretty rare spectrum of choices for most people, but they were influenced by my past.

I grew up with my younger brother and three older cousins practically on the same New York block, living the normal life of football, fighting, partying, but we came from a somewhat military family. My dad had been in the Army and I had an uncle in the Coast Guard and another in the Navy. One grandfather had been a bombardier while the other worked the Brooklyn naval shipyards. After leaving the military, my dad became a federal agent, and built a thirty-year career as an inspector with the U.S. Postal Service. He travelled often, working fraud cases and the like, and he was sorely missed.

Though Dad never pushed the idea of service on my younger brother or myself, some of the imagined dramatic element definitely seeped into my mind. Our culture with TV especially glorifies the military and of course these men and women deserve our respect, but for me I was very ignorant as to what the real military was going to be like.

As I wrestled with how to turn my life around, my mom, a somewhat unique traditional Irish/Italian-American housewife and teacher, wanted me to stay in New York to remain close by (like the amazing mother she is!), and my dad was more open to me joining the military. But, ultimately, they were both supportive no matter what I chose.

I think that he was proud of the fact that I was considering the military but he didn't push me to go in either direction. I guess the service was in my blood because I made the decision to join the military over the Peace Corps and grad school. I expected enlisting would be hard but I looked forward to it. I wanted to be a hero, to help people, protect them, and save their lives.

What I learned about the military later on is that it's not

about that. I went to boot camp in Chicago and then to intelligence training school in Virginia. After that, it was on to Coronado, an island off the coast of San Diego, for Basic Underwater Demolition School (BUDS), which is Special Forces training for Navy Seals. I'm not sure if I thought it was ever truly a mistake but almost immediately after boot camp began, I definitely knew it wasn't what I had hoped for and dreamt of. Boot camp was almost the same thing every day—the schedule was very regimented and predictable. Think Groundhog Day!

When you are in boot camp you cannot legally leave the base without permission. If you do, they put you in jail. Essentially, you, your life and body become the property of the United States government.

This really started to become an issue for me because I was used to traveling whenever I wanted. I was the kind of person who went wherever I felt like going at that moment, literally, and to go from that level of freedom to needing permission to make every move was a tough transition for me.

There were other things too. I had no idea and to what degree, how cold, hard, and just how downright nasty the culture of the military could be. I never expected discrimination on so many levels. It was very racially divided: whites stuck with whites, blacks with blacks, Southerners with Southerners and so forth. I had more than a little trouble with a group of Good Ol' Boys from the South who didn't like a 'Yankee' being in their squad.

Before boot camp, I hadn't been aware that in southern states such as Texas, Florida and Alabama judges gave some convicts the option of going to the military instead of jail for a first offense. There were around a dozen men in my boot camp class from really, really depressed areas who had turned to crime and formed gangs to try to make some money.

As I got to know them, I realized they weren't bad people, but I still had to break up all sorts of fights, including one involving knives. I had to carry someone on my back to an ambulance, just having slit his wrists in an attempt to kill himself, and I witnessed more mental breakdowns in three months than I ever have in my entire life.

I tried to take a back seat and just be the quiet guy in the corner, but the people in charge had other plans for me. At boot camp, there were close to a hundred young men, and at age twenty-five I was one of the oldest. There were two or three people who were older than me and a few around my age, but the rest of them were in their late teens and early twenties. The brass noticed my age and the fact that I scored in the 98th percentile in aptitude tests, plus I had a college degree.

So they brought me in for an interview, told me they thought I had the best leadership qualities in the group, and promptly put me in charge of these hundred young men.

The Honeymoon Is Over

The difference between the reality of the military and the way it is promoted on TV and in the media really disillusioned me. I'd come to it feeling very patriotic and thinking it would be really hard but somewhat glamorous, if I was up to the task. However, that isn't true for 99.9% of all people who go into the military. It is an extremely hard job to face every day. There's a huge disparity between how enlisted men and women live, compared to how the officers live. The hours and the intensity of the work are on overload, and you are expected to perform without complaint. It was frustrating for me because if I had waited to go to OCS (Officer Candidate School), I could have had a much easier and possibly more enjoyable time.

After boot camp, I went to Virginia Beach, VA, and studied at U.S. Naval Intelligence for six months, learning about aircraft, ships, how to read satellite imagery and learning military strategies. I'd bought the hype they sold, thinking it would be about protection, and here I was instead, basically learning how to become the aggressor.

Being a driven person, I did my best to keep up, doing all the different tasks asked of me, including the physical ones: obstacle courses, running, swimming, push-ups and various calisthenics throughout the day. We were not allowed to walk; instead, we had to jog everywhere we went. SEAL training is an intense process for sure, a huge shift from my previous life.

Then came my first injury, a torn groin and that was the beginning of the dark night of the soul for me. I was out of the training program for the time being. I had worked so hard and for so long. I had literally trained for over two years to have achieved this unique opportunity, but now I could feel it all slipping away.

On the outside I kept cool but inside I was having a rough time of it. I felt terrible - it was an absolute nightmare for me. For the first time in my life I had no friends, no family; no one who could watch my back. I was in some very serious pain for weeks after that first injury.

Once I started to heal, I began drinking too much and going to nasty military bars off-base, brawling and challenging some pretty mean dudes. I have never been a big guy, or the toughest guy, but I had practiced martial arts for many years and could be a fast-to-anger and ferocious opponent. I viewed the fighting as an outlet.

After my leg was well enough, it was right back to all the

intense training but after a while my body began to sustain injuries from all the abuse I was putting it through. First, the constant jogging did a number on my knees. Then, once again, I injured my groin, which required me to undergo a period of recuperation that I didn't really obey.

Even as I was healing, I was still training. Anyone who's been in the program knows that even when you're hurt, you still have to train, but I couldn't train my lower body, so instead I spent hours and hours working on my upper body. I pushed myself, despite the groin injury, because that was the mindset of everyone around me, to make the ultimate effort at all times. If you're not working very hard, you're not going to make it.

Even though I couldn't run, I continued to work out my upper body, hoping that when my groin healed I would only have to boost my lower body strength to catch up. So for the next few weeks, that was the main way I spent my time.

I was really starting to get into it when my shoulders gave out. One day while at the training pool, me and the other guys were getting a 'beat down' by some of the instructors. I won't go into some of the worst stories, but this particular day was still awful for me. I was pretty decent at pull ups and could definitely pump out twenty to twenty-five at one time. One of the instructors, who seemed to take a real 'liking' to me, told me to put down my crutches, hop over to the pull up bars and to "give him twenty".

I did this, but then he proceeded to have me do push-ups, squat thrusts, and more, over and over while the rest of the class was swimming in the pool. About forty minutes later, I was having trouble maintaining consciousness—it was really hot that day, it had to be over ninety degrees. He then got me back up on the pull up bar and told me to keep going until he told me to stop. I carried on but would have to stop and rest now and then.

When I came off the bar he told me get straight back up, and he continued to do this over and over, to the point when I couldn't even hang on the bar. My shoulders felt like someone was sticking a hot poker inside them. I heard pops and felt searing pain in my neck and down my arms, eventually collapsing into a heap under the bars, writhing in pain.

The instructor walked over to me and said to one of the other instructors, "I thought you said he was a NY tough guy?" He shook his head in disgust and walked away, leaving me there.

At that precise moment in time, I was officially broken, mentally, physically and emotionally. Doctors told me that I had a separated AC joint, impingement on the tendons in both shoulders, bursitis, tendonitis and all sorts of scar tissue and more going on with my shoulders.

For weeks, I couldn't wash my face or brush my teeth without being in extreme pain—any movement involving me having to tighten up my arms or shoulders was extremely difficult. It was near impossible to shower and it took an hour to dress myself; the simple act of putting on and tying my boots could be fifteen minutes of excruciating pain. Sometimes I did not know if my tears were from pain, depression or simply from pure exasperation.

Transitions

As I am sure it is obvious after reading the above, the pain got so bad that I was told by the powers that be I couldn't continue. I turned to more alcohol to numb the pain, both physical and emotional. I could barely face the realization that I was no longer going to have the chance to be a Special Forces team member, a lifelong dream of mine, but instead was going to be forced into the regular Navy service and put on a ship for six months at a time. I wouldn't be going down the officer route but would have to wait a year or possibly more to be approved to go to Officer Candidate School.

So here I was, at twenty-seven years old with a college degree, a broken body, a broken heart and at one of the lowest spots you can be in a military career, essentially committed to spending several more years on a boat with no control over my career or the direction I was going. The harsh, cold reality slapped my face: I had signed my life away to Uncle Sam and was going to be away from family and friends for six months to a year at a time, literally across the world, on an aircraft carrier with four or five thousand other guys. Not my idea of a good time.

To keep me fit for duty, military doctors decided that I should have reconstructive surgery on my shoulders, but I was uneasy with the idea. I got a second opinion, that of the family doctor who confirmed my position; that it was wholly unnecessary. The fact that I had almost undergone a serious operation that a respected doctor thought wasn't appropriate at all left me seething. I ended up refusing the reconstructive shoulder surgery, which turned out to be a major blessing.

I didn't know so at the time, but there's a loophole in the military: If you refuse to have the surgery that they deem necessary, they can't force you to go under the knife but neither can they indefinitely keep you on light duty. They therefore have to grant you a medical discharge, and that's what happened with me.

I had mixed feelings: on one hand, I was depressed and

not happy at all in the military, but on the other hand, becoming a SEAL team member and an officer had been a goal of mine for many years and now it all felt like a tremendous waste of time.

In the lowest depths, I spent an entire night drinking Jack Daniels by myself, at home crying, throwing things and staring at the wall. This was definitely one of the darkest nights of my soul. It wasn't my first and it certainly would not be my last. I was feeling tortured on so many levels, I was lonely, I was scared, I was in pain. I had no idea what to do or who to reach out to. I had a great family and friends back in NY, but I didn't feel like anyone could understand. I was embarrassed at my perceived failure and not reaching my goals. I was hideously depressed and at one point, I just fell to my knees. It was the absolute bottom of my whole experience up to that point.

Down on my painful knees, my shoulders aching all the time, tears streaming down my face, I asked for help in a way that I had never asked for it before. I felt like I had no hope left. "I don't know where else to turn; there isn't anyone in my life right now who I can reach out to who can help me with this, and I don't know what else to do. If there is a God, please help me." I begged God for help with all that I had in heart. I remember saying, "If you even exist..."

I remember that phrase clearly, because I exhorted an incoherent ramble for about fifteen minutes, just asking for help on my knees, crying to beat the band. I exhausted myself and ended up barely making it to bed and passing out immediately.

The next morning before my eyes even opened, I knew something was different. What?! No hangover? Feeling good? The feeling that I had when I woke up was such a huge change from the norm, and quantum leaps away from where I had been the night before. It was as if I had gone to bed as one person and had awakened as another.

My bedroom had a sliding glass door that led onto a balcony and the early morning sun was blazing in my eyes. It felt so warm and loving. I had the most amazing feeling of relief, of being safe and of something I had not felt in a long time...hope. It was a one hundred and eighty-degree difference from the way I had felt the night before, and to this day, I don't know specifically what changed things. I didn't hear God's voice, I didn't see any angels, and all I knew was that something in me had been transformed. I had a radically different feeling; I knew I had been in contact with grace, love, and somehow had been helped while I slept. I had been healed miraculously from where I was the night before.

From that point on, I never doubted the power of prayer and the power of asking for help. It was that day right then, that my whole outlook on life changed. Before I had pitied myself because it had seemed a really big step to leave the comforts of New York and the lifestyle that I had been leading behind, and I had been considering my time spent in the armed forces as a huge loss. Not just physically, but emotionally.

Now I realized my time in service had exposed me to many other walks of life. I had gotten to know and care for people from parts of the country I had never seen and lifestyles I had never known about. I knew how much I had been challenged and how much I had grown as a man, as a shipmate, a human being. I realized that to some extent, growing up in Long Island had been a sheltered kind of 'dream life' and my years in military service had been a useful and necessary shock to my system.

Often we can't see at the time that the pain we are experiencing is really what we need to turn things around and start living a life that's truer to ourselves, with more possibilities and much more enjoyable.

The Turning Point

As I accepted and reconciled that I would be leaving the Navy, I began coming out of my depression and feeling extremely inspired about what was going to happen. The last six weeks were great. I knew I was going to have a medical discharge and was just waiting for the papers to come through. I'd have to get signatures from a few offices but other than that, I was out! THANK GOD (Especially now that I felt reconnected to God in a way I had never known)! Gratitude was quickly becoming my saving grace.

I went back and forth between feeling a huge relief and worrying that they might somehow find a way to keep me in the Navy. Looking back now, I am able to see how perfectly it all unfolded. I could not be 'free' until I set myself free by asking, seeking and accepting help. It's a good thing to remember that help is always available and that all we need to do is ask for it.

Meanwhile, because I was on light duty, I was able to get a part time job once my shoulders healed enough. I got a job at Bay Books, the quaintest and coolest little beachside bookstore in Coronado, CA, and immediately became best friends with the owner. Shirley was in her late sixties, a woman of German descent, was although she was born in Mexico, where she spent most of her years. She looked out for me like a surrogate mother and wanted me to call her Aunt Shirley!

I was so glad to have that feeling of family again, after being so long without it. To this day when I think of the kindness, generosity and all-round goodness of this woman, it makes my heart sing. If it wasn't too busy around the store, she encouraged us employees to browse, read and really get to know the books so we could better sell them to customers. She was a progressive thinker and wanted us to ensconce ourselves in the material so that we could talk intelligently about the books we were selling.

Shirley also had an apartment available at her beautiful house into which I moved to get off the military base and enjoyed my first taste of not living the military way in years. Woo hoo! I had to be at the military base for four to six hours a day, but that was it, nothing compared to the 24/7 of the last two years.

That change really lifted my spirits. My appreciation was overflowing to new heights and I was marveling at how quickly my life had changed once I had broken down and asked for help. Being in this bookstore was one of the best things that could have happened to me. I had access to all this amazing information that I had always been passionate about but had never really dedicated myself to, things like philosophy, religion, self-development and spirituality.

I started diving into all these books on my breaks and was able to borrow some to take home as well. I was placed in charge of those sections because I was so passionate about the topics and I started reading for hours and hours every day. Not only did I start reading, but I was also doing the exercises, filling out the workbooks and following the instructions of Deepak Chopra, Louise Hay, Wayne Dyer, Tony Robbins, Emerson, Thoreau, The Dalai Lama, Thich Nhat Hanh, Daniel Goleman, and Dan Millman, just to name a few. I was so inspired by the material that I started taking local classes as well.

I took up yoga and started going for massages, as my shoulders needed a lot of work. I had acupuncture, indulging in all of these holistic treatments, and meeting amazing people who treated me so wonderfully. My spirit started moving, and I said, "Wow, there is really something going on here."

I felt my heart start to open to other possibilities for my life post-navy. Even though I had some serious injuries, I was confident that I would heal with some patience, love and good help from acupuncturists, massage therapists, yoga and meditation teachers, and herbalists. I really got into supplements and herbs to further the healing process, which was a tremendous enlightening experience. I was meditating two or three hours a day, working part time, surfing, going to Buddhist meditation retreats, and enjoying more time in nature, outdoors, at the beach and in the mountains.

My consciousness was changing, because I was living my life differently. I was dedicated to the practices that I knew I needed to change my life inside-out. I knew I never wanted to be that guy again with Jack Daniels on his lap wondering if I could make it, so I refused to dwell on that experience. I started praying, meditating and being thankful for what I had been given and really opening my mind and heart to new ways of thinking. I knew I had been given a second chance and I wanted to make the best of it.

A benefit of the nightclub life I lived before was that I had been able to save a lot of money. Now, with some help from my generous and loving parents I could afford to work just a bit and still cover my meagre expenses. Now I could afford to work just a bit and still cover my meagre expenses. It was a very self-sufficient time for me and everything seemed to come together for this purpose. I did a lot of hiking and camping, got into nature, explored the desert, mountains and the beach.

I remember one seminal moment when I was hiking alone

in the Cuyamaca Mountains and came face to face with a huge buck on the trail. His antlers were some of the biggest I had ever seen. He sure did not look like the normal deer I was used to seeing in the area. He and I stared at one another for what felt like forever, neither of us moving or making any noise. I was surprised but not fearful, just relaxed, breathed and kept his gaze, really allowing his majestic presence to wash over me.

After what must have been at least a minute or two, he turned and silently disappeared into the brush. I have never had quite that kind of experience since. Truly beautiful! It was a healing time for me on so many levels.

My life started to open up to some completely different areas which I had never considered before. I was so inspired by all the knowledge I was gaining! I didn't know exactly what I wanted to do or how, but I knew that I somehow wanted to work with people, to help them grasp the practice of really developing ourselves as human beings and teaching them to grow.

Anyone experiencing a time of intense transition and transformation knows it often doesn't happen in an instant and you often *ping-pong* between the two states of optimism and misery. That's how it happened for me. I was a week out from being discharged when a college buddy of mine came to visit from New York. I took the day off so we were just hanging out, walking down this beach street, having a good old time.

We came upon a couple fighting outside a little boutique clothes store. This guy in his late twenties was yelling at a younger girl in a very aggressive way. That's something I've never approved of. She was in her late teens, with long brown hair and looked like the surfer girl next door. He was in her face, things were escalating and I could tell she was scared. I didn't know them, but I couldn't help myself. I walked straight up, interrupted their argument and basically told him to beat it. Luckily, he didn't seem interested in pursuing the matter with me and left.

The girl was crying, so my friend and I just hung out with her for a few minutes to make sure she was okay. She said that she was really grateful that I'd stepped in. It transpired that the guy was an ex-boyfriend of hers who had kind of lost his mind.

After recovering a bit, she invited us to hang out with her and her friends at a bonfire party that night. They turned out to be a great group of guys and girls and we seemed to form an immediate friendship when we met.

I found myself in a really good space that night, owing to our new friends and my buddy from New York, and I felt really happy and appreciated in a way that I hadn't for some time. I was also feeling some intense emotions from being in such a state of transition. I knew my old life was gone forever and I was expanding into this completely new direction.

I had already gone from a nightclub, party-hearty lifestyle, making a lot of cash in New York, to the military. Now I was coming out of the military. I was injured but at the same time feeling more spiritual and emotional, with my heart expanding more than it ever had before.

I was unsure what this all meant for me. But, I was at this bonfire party with about fifteen other people, just hanging out and playing music. There were some different things going on; some heavy partying, which made me uncomfortable. I wasn't in that mode, and especially didn't want to jeopardize my medical discharge, so I decided to go for a walk down the beach instead.

As I walked along the sand, I started to pray as if God was

right next to me. I was still learning to be comfortable with it. Previously I had always questioned whether there was a God, and I wasn't sure how I felt about a Source, the Universe, or whether there was any organizing principle whatsoever.

Things had recently changed for me in that respect, with the sunlight experience, and now I began to feel comfortable starting up a conversation with God, so to speak. I did, however, still ask for some sort of sign. Was I making up all of the spiritual awakening in my head, just to make myself feel better? Was I latching on to whatever was some sort of salve for my broken heart, my depression? I needed a sign from God to know if I was going in the right direction. I really wanted to know if...

Well, in the middle of that conversation with God, out of nowhere, a guy appeared. I hadn't seen him approach, although I *was* walking on a dark, lonely stretch of beach.

"Hey," he said.

He was taller than me, slim with brown hair and probably in his early thirties. A desperate air clung to him; he seemed nervous, tense, and distress radiated off him in waves. He seemed to be at the end of his rope.

He asked what I was doing, and I replied that I was at a party, indicating the fire half a mile down the beach. He was apparently looking for drugs. I told him that I was in the military and didn't have anything for him. but suggested he could probably smoke with the kids at the party.

He replied that he was looking for something strong. He seemed very distraught, and while I felt uncomfortable. I didn't want to be rude to a guy who was clearly in a tough spot.

I was in this great emotional space, in this great heart space, and I just opened up and asked, "Hey, what's going on, man?" I wasn't trying to be his therapist; I just didn't want to be a jerk.

He turned, looked me right in the face and replied, "You really want to know?"

At that moment, I was pretty nervous I may be getting into something scary, but something made me continue. "Sure, I have a few minutes."

We ended up going over to a bench and chatting. He turned out to be a really nice guy, just going through an extremely tough time. His wife and children had been tragically killed in a car accident just a couple of weeks before, and he'd come out to California from Ohio to get away and to have some time to himself, to process that horrific experience.

He told me he had made the decision to take his life that night, and that he had planned to do it through a drug overdose. His grief was palpable, and while I could not relate anywhere near to his level of tragedy, I explained to him that I too, had just come out of a really dark place, and that if I had succeeded, anybody could come out of it because I had at times felt close to making some very ill-advised decisions myself.

I explained how I had put myself in dangerous and negative situations because of anger, sadness and depression, but that within a handful of months, I had been able to transform it without the need for a therapist or spiritual guide.

"How did you do it?" he asked.

I told him in truth that there were many different factors to coping, but there was one really simple one that made the most dramatic difference for me: simply *gratitude*.

I used the techniques I'm going to show you in this book to completely turn my life around. I explained to him that even though so many of us have tough, sad stories to tell, we still have wonderful, amazing divine gifts acquired from our past, and still have those gifts now in our current life situations. Its just a matter of finding them, recognising them and remembering them. I talked with him about how I started looking for what I was grateful for more than what I was sad about. Just performing that simple exercise completely transformed my life and the person I am.

I shared some of these insights with this gentleman and we ended up talking for over two hours that night on the beach. At the end, we hugged like best friends and amazingly, he told me that I had saved his life. I hadn't realized that I had this profound effect on him. I thought I was just talking to someone earnestly and sharing my life.

But by the sheer act of sharing my story, he received help and received a glimmer of hope for the future. The look on his face was resolute.

Of course, he still had a tough road ahead but seemed to acknowledge that he was going to be okay at some point down the road.

Unbeknownst to him, he gave me a huge gift that night, and to this day, I consider it one of the most amazing experiences I've ever had.

As I walked back to the party, feeling elated and very strange at the same time, I realized I had received my sign and hadn't even realized it at the time! I didn't catch the connection at all until afterwards and then I just started jumping into the air and spinning around. I didn't know what to do with myself, I was so ecstatic because all of a sudden it had become clear.

I looked up at the night sky, the moon and the stars, and at my favorite constellation, Orion, and said, "thank you, thank you, thank you."

I was lifted up, really and truly. It was one of the happiest moments of my life. It was so clear to me that I received my sign from God, my message. The words "ask and you shall receive" echoed in my head, and I think that is true for anyone. Any one of us can ask for a sign, for help, for support or divine guidance.

When the request comes from our truest selves, the answer is on its way. The real question is, "do you have the eyes to see the answer?"

At that precise moment, thankfully, I *did* have the eyes to see it. There is always an opportunity available if you search for it. You must focus on it, expect it and have faith in it. For this, you don't need to spend twenty years in a monastery; you can reach out to God, your Creator, The Source, The Force, whatever term you would like to use, for help anytime, 24/7, with intention, an open mind and a grateful heart.

That's why I love the gratitude process! It is one of the simplest techniques to grasp, one which has a quick, sometimes immediate, and profound effect on our lives. If we stay aware and open to what comes through, it can be our guiding light. I know it is for me.

As I continued to explore gratitude and the act of appreciation more deeply, I was often shocked and amazed at the results. I began to question the process of becoming more conscious about my life. Even though I felt more connected and aware of my spirit, the skeptic in me remained.

Despite many amazing experiences with my consciousness expanding and the gratitude process working time after time, I still reverted to old patterns at times, taking steps backwards. I struggled with thoughts like, "Oh sure, I have great connections with those I love, but I don't have the relationships I'd hoped to have with them," and, "I have close friends, but they don't even know me anymore because I have changed so much over the last couple of years," "I've been blessed with a beautiful, smart, loving girlfriend, but she doesn't really appreciate me the way I want to be appreciated," and so on.

On many occasions it was a battle to bring myself back to base and negative thoughts would creep in, preventing me from allowing the good feelings from flowing, but the main thing is, I kept at it!

Despite feeling somewhat isolated at the beginning of the process and doubtful that it would work long term, each time I told myself I would try the exercise anyway. Afterwards, when I felt better, I'd be confused as to how that happened. I knew that help came because I asked for it, I just didn't get why.

As I look back now at those experiences that occurred almost 20 years ago, I realize what changed for me. A little seed of faith had been planted in me that was not there before – a tiny particle of belief that I could get help, not from a person, not from outside myself, but from within, from Spirit, a belief which revitalized me.

To this day, the experiences of that sunlit morning and the beach party are some of the most powerful in my life. They helped me to see the world, my life, and their possibilities differently. My hope is that this book can be one of the opportunities that support *you* in your life to get closer to whatever it is you hold most dear, whatever you desire most, to gain, live, and experience your highest potential.

Your Turn

As you can see, in just over a year, I went from being in one of the worst times of my life to being happier than ever, living a life that was completely carefree. I learned how to surf, meditate,, enjoyed all sorts of spiritual experiences, workshops, and I was keeping in great shape at the same time by running every morning, hiking and doing yoga and tai chi. I was generally feeling spectacular about my life.

At the age of twenty-seven, I was still relatively young, unmarried, with no kids, no debt and no responsibility. Furthermore, I had more money than I needed in the bank. For the first time I was actually getting to know the *real* me and finding out what I wanted to do with the rest of my life.

This sparked a whole new direction for me. I attended a holistic college, where I studied for three years. I was really drawn to Buddhism to, and studied at a Buddhist temple for two years, taking classes on meditation and going on weekend retreats. It really was a wonderful, spectacular time.

Around this time, I was introduced to "The Work" as taught by G.I. Gurdjieff, and began learning about Esoteric Christianity, Sufism, Hinduism, Presence, Consciousness and the potential of the human being. I have never looked back.

During the last fifteen plus years, I have studied a wide range of topics pertaining to Positive Psychology, including the amazing effects of Gratitude, Appreciation, Awareness, Self-Love and Forgiveness, to name but a few.

All because I had experienced a depressed state, this beautiful life suddenly seemed to have so much to offer. My resistance, doubt, fear and worry all yearned to be replaced with its opposite emotion in me. No matter where we are in life, that unwanted situation or feeling can be transmuted into exactly what we are hoping for, and wishing to see and experience in our lives.

Does this sound like something you would like to experience? If so, how can you have the same or similar experiences? Throughout this book, you'll discover what it means to lead your life from a place of gratitude and deep appreciation. This is merely the beginning.

By starting here, all else will become possible. Grace will descend upon you and your life, because when we are truly grateful, not just going through the motions and saying the words, but actually feeling them, we become aligned with our Higher Self, the Divine in us. You can change your whole perception, your circumstances and your awareness with one simple question: What are you grateful for and what do you appreciate at this very moment?

In this book, I'll walk you through my process and show you how to acquire and express gratitude. For example, I love to go on, as Abraham-Hicks refers to it, a "Rampage of Appreciation," where I build a list of all the things I am grateful for in my life. I start off with the people—my wife, my son, my parents, my brother, his family, my cousins, close friends, co-workers, clients and all those I love the most. Then I concentrate on the things I am grateful for—the fact that we were expecting a baby when I began this writing, and that we now have a beautiful, healthy happy boy, Patrick!

The baby is doing well and so is my wife. She is so supportive, as are my family, friends and co-workers! When you get through the first group of people, usually close family and friends, I pick out less obvious individuals and focus on their qualities and imagine their faces. I picture them smiling, so it's almost as if I am with them in my mind.

Sometimes it's people who have sadly departed this world (like my Aunt Rose, who is the best).I just picture their smiling, happy faces, and love them at that moment and appreciate them—our relationship, the goodness we have shared and I'm instantly lifted up by that experience. I am lifted to a new perspective, a higher place from where I can view my life and view the experience of life itself. I feel more aligned with my life purpose in these moments, more in touch with my life and the lives of those I love most.

As I continue to move on through the process, I'm reminded that it's not just about people, it's about all the things, situations and experiences I am grateful for. I also like to think about the interconnection of all the people and things, the Oneness that life truly is. These thoughts open my mind and heart.

I think about my business, not just the awesome people working in and for it, my amazing clients, but about all the different aspects that help to make my business function and remain successful, such as technology, computers and social media and all the things they involve.

I am grateful for other things too, things often taken for granted, like having a car that works and being able to drive my wife to the hospital when we have our baby, and for the baby seat that we received as a generous gift at the baby shower and all the other gifts from that event.

I am grateful that we are working with good, smart, compassionate doctors. One good thought leads to another good, appreciative thought, and as this exercise continues, I realize that eventually I can do this automatically without having to make a concerted effort to carry out the process. After practicing this for years, one really interesting aspect I have noticed is that it is as though the thoughts are not actually emanating *from* me, rather they seem to be passing *through* me, from a place I am connected to.

I even extend the process to things I haven't yet physically experienced! That's kind of like graduate school for people who practice gratitude, but the good news is you don't have to study the subject for years and years like one has to do in regular academia. It's really about reminding ourselves that anything is possible.

If you believe this and start practicing it, you will start to see how powerfully it works, and you will start to draw in and attract experiences based on the fact that the Law of Attraction works continuously in our lives twenty-four hours a day.. This means what we think about we bring about, what we resist persists, and what we focus on grows. Therefore, if I am focusing on love and gratitude and all the things that I appreciate, I know that during those moments I am bringing them more significantly into my life. Alternatively, if I am worried, doubtful, full of anxiety or desperate, guess what? I get more of that!

A New Plan

This book provides you with some of the basic tools capable of changing your life. This is not a false claim or wishful thinking. What I realized all those years ago in the dark night of my soul, and subsequently relearned many times since, was that I didn't possess the tools to feel better early on in my life. I was not taught how to manage my emotions. I was not taught how to become aware of my breath, to ground myself, to calm myself, and to infuse appreciation into my life, but anyone can learn this.

Once you've finished this book, you'll be equipped with the same tools and techniques I used to turn my life around. I've included all of the preliminary information you need to grasp in order to facilitate the process, and I'm sharing the scientific foundation for everything I'll be recommending, so you don't have to take just my word for it. I'm providing you with specific exercises you can use to quickly transform your mental state and attain some level of peace and happiness.

Each exercise that I give will mostly only take a few minutes to complete, so, if you need to heal your life, the couple of minutes you dedicate to the process will make the investment of time you have made reading this book well worth the effort.

Coaching will also be provided on how to incorporate the practice of gratitude into your daily life and circumstances, so you don't feel you have to go to the mountaintop to access the benefits. There's even a section for skeptics in order to help troubleshoot the practice. Imagine me right there beside you, like the sign for which I asked God. This book can be your sign if choose to make it so.

It's my wish you use this book primarily to learn how to feel better. When we feel better in this life, we make better decisions for ourselves and for others.

When we are confident and full of faith, hope, joy and love, we make much better decisions than when we are in doubt, fearful, confused, angry, sad, or experiencing hateful thoughts of revenge or violence. We make better decisions for ourselves and for the rest of humanity when we are just happy, so I hope this book will help people to feel better and to enjoy their lives more, by giving them the tools to be able to put all of this appreciation into practice.

Once you've incorporated these practices into your life over a period of time, you won't have to think about how to do it, as the process will become automatic and part of your natural way of being.

You'll get to know the process inside and out, but this book will equip you with tools you can use for many years, as well as share with other people. Tell your friends, your family, your children; in fact, tell anyone you care about, because these guidelines are so simple that we can all practice them.

Now here's where I want to share: just how grateful I feel to be able to get this information out. It feels magnificent to share and I appreciate *you* for reading this book, because of the results you'll see and the amazing opportunity that gratitude and appreciation produces for us all.

Chapter 1

Power to Choose Your Thoughts

"Let us be grateful to people who make us happy; they are the charming gardeners who make our souls blossom."
--Marcel Proust

The Key to Changing Your Life

In order to affect your life positively, you must understand the extreme level of power you possess over your emotions, thoughts and the feelings that result. We always, 100% of the time, without question, have the power to choose what we are going to think. Always. This is both a belief I have and a practice I've experienced.

If you don't have that belief, It will seem that this statement is false. However, if you just dip a toe into that idea, just a little bit, just the tip of the big toe, you can test it out and find out for yourself if you find it to be true! As you explore this idea with the explanations in this chapter, you're almost always going to be given some evidence that it's true. The more we practice the idea that we have the power to choose our thoughts, which means we get to have the power to choose how we end up feeling, which means we get to choose the emotional tone of our experiences, the better off we will be in our lifetime.

I can't say that we can just visualize the exact thing that we want to experience and picture everybody at the party wearing blue petticoats. That's not the way it will happen, but what will happen is that we'll start to see a lot more blue than what we expected.

Life isn't this exact science—it's more of an art form, it's something that has surprises and beautiful opportunities around every corner. We have the opportunity to fall in love with the mystery of life, and this in itself can be—and certainly has been for me—one of life's greatest joys. We're going down the rabbit hole when we tap in to this kind of philosophy, but I wouldn't have it any other way. I love knowing that I have the power to choose my thoughts every single time about any subject in any situation.

I don't care if there is a gun pointed at my head, the truth is that I have the power to choose my thoughts in that moment. I have the power to choose fear, anger, hate, or have the power to choose divinity, love and beauty, regardless of the outer circumstances. This is an advanced way of thinking, but you have access to the same level of control over your thoughts.

My Path

I was introduced to the power of choosing your thoughts through the work of Louise Hay, of "Heal Your Life" fame, and the Crazy Wisdom Teacher, George Ivanovich Gurdjieff. Gurdjieff, who was born in the late 1800's at the border between Turkey and Russia, was interested in finding out about the powers of the Universe and the truth about spirituality from a very young age, because he was born in a very religious area. It was a hotbed of religious fervor and this inspired him to explore Christianity, Islam and Judaism. He set out to find out what was what in the world as far as 'consciousness', and he went through the Middle East, Russia and Europe studying with all sorts of spiritual master teachers.

There is an interesting book entitled, *Meetings with Remarkable Men*, that I think is worth reading if you enjoy studying spiritual teacher stories and experiences.

One of the things he found out to be true through his study of how the mind works was that you could stop thoughts. That intrigued me. I wondered, "How could someone stop thoughts? What would it be like if my mind could be perfectly serene? What would my relationships be like if I could be calmer in stressful moments? What kind of a person would I be if I could be more loving and compassionate? What would the opportunities of my life be like if I were able to do something like 'stop thought'?"

My mind was flooded with all the possibilities, and my inspiration was sparked; to tell you the truth, I have never looked back. Based on the concept of 'stopping thought', it became a goal of mine to have much more control over my mind. I explored meditation and different mindfulness exercises to come up with ways to manipulate the flow of my thoughts, to have the power to choose them or just stopping them altogether so that I could get a break.

That's what really happens when our thoughts calm down: we take a break from our "monkey mind". The monkey mind asks, "What am I going to do next, where am I going, what just happened?" This surface mindset is where the ego takes control and really directs your thoughts.

Through the years, I explored the power of thought, the power to have command of mind, being able to focus and to direct one's thoughts, which of course leads us into very different experiences and ideas, based on the thoughts we are thinking and the emotions we are feeling.

These practices are a significantly different way of living in the world. It often affects people so profoundly that they may never think the same way ever again.

Whenever I'm reading powerful spiritual literature, I will pull out one quote or idea and take a really long walk to digest the experience. On one of these walks, I was pondering the quote, "The kingdom of heaven is within." And that idea, ever since the first time I read it, really made a strong impression on me.

I used that idea, that saying, that quote from Jesus and others, as I went on my walk. I was gone for two hours, and at some point in the walk, I stopped dead in my tracks. What came to me was that one of the aspects of this Kingdom of Heaven was that we have the power to choose our thoughts. When this correlation came through to me, my whole body became electric, with pins, needles and chills running up and down my spine. I was sweating from walking for so long, even though it was cold out.

It was a perfect winter day in late February. It was about 25-30 degrees and the sun was setting, around 4pm here in New York. I walked for another hour because I needed to process this mind-expanding idea.

The Kingdom of Heaven is where our power resides and one of the aspects of this power is that we can direct our own minds. To me, the Kingdom of Heaven means many things, but in the context of this book, it is the place we want to connect to inside ourselves that reveals our true essence, beauty and strength. We may not realize it, but we do this by what we say, the stories we tell ourselves, by what we repeat to ourselves, by watching our patterns of thought and then attempting to change them, or catching ourselves in a pattern and saying, "No, wait. I know where this pattern leads. I don't want to go in that direction because it doesn't lead to somewhere good. I am going to lead myself in this direction, and I believe it is going to lead me somewhere better."

For me, some of the things that happened as a result of this breakthrough were subtle but astounding. I was having some trouble with someone I once worked with, a great, amazing human being, but we clashed over the way he spoke to me, the way he treated me, and his whole business approach, which was full of a 'fear, lack and scarcity'-type of mindset.

I decided to apply the idea that I could access the Highest in Me from the Kingdom of Heaven during our clashes. When I would get angry at him, I would think, "Okay, so what is the opposite of getting angry at him? For the most part, that is loving, right?"

Before I entered a meeting with him, I would think and feel loving thoughts towards him. "If it weren't for him, this project probably wouldn't have come off in this way." "I really do just love this business." "I know he's had some tough things in his life, so I am going to send him some love and compassion around that."

I chose to stop following what some teachers call 'circling thoughts'. This is when people essentially become crystallized in their patterns because they never think outside the box. They think within the grooves that they have in their mind. They can never really be different people because those circling thoughts are always happening and they are believing those thoughts are them.

We need to be aware of these thought patterns before we are able to take advantage of this new way of thinking, especially when we judge someone as wrong, bad, untrustworthy, criminal, etc. Choosing to think a different thought shows we are jumping out of that groove and creating a new potential for our lives, relationships and opportunities.

When I started doing this exercise, going from anger in the moment, pivoting my mind from one place to another, from a place of resentment and anger to a place of love and gratitude, the results were overwhelming. During the first attempts, I thought, "This is hooey. I'm still pissed off, this isn't working."

But as continued the practice, I felt better, even though I wasn't seeing tangible results in the physical world. I just felt better internally, so on that basis, I concluded that this was a practice worth pursuing.

I repeated the process a few times over that week, and one instance was particularly powerful. I was on my drive into work and I knew my coworker would be at the office. I began to exude love for him before I even got out of my car to go into work. As I walked in the door, he got up from his desk and walked over to me, something he never did before in over 2 years of working together. He usually barely looked up from his computer when I walked in.

He wasn't a morning person so he'd grumble, "Good morning," and not even look in my direction. Looking back, this was another pet peeve that I fed into, which helped me remain unhappy about my relationship with him.

But instead of his usual greeting that morning, he got up from his desk and he walked over to me. He said, "You know, I gotta tell you, we've been dealing with a lot of stress and we've been so busy. What do you think about talking a half a day? I want to buy you lunch."

I just looked at him, since he'd never spoken to me that way before. I thought, "Holy shit! It worked!" I finally got the vibration high enough to effect the physical world.

It wasn't that I was manipulating him; I tapped into the love that was in him. Because we went through quite a bit together as coworkers, I knew how big his heart was and what a great guy he really was. He just didn't express it in all the ways I wanted him to at our jobs.

Energy and attraction is all about alignment, and people can't feel our love unless we are really vibrating it sincerely and authentically. From there, it's because we are essentially all one. That is part of my philosophy: every single human being on the planet is part of the same material, connected in some way, and when we are able to tap into the highest vibration, it somehow dematerializes the perceived obstacles between us and then creates new ways for us to communicate and connect.

There is a phenomenon coined by Gregg Braden as the "Divine Matrix", by others as "The Field" or the "The Ethers", but all it really means is this energetic system that we, God, and all of the physical world is connected to and a part of. We interact with this system through the thoughts we think and the emotions we feel, vibrating on specific frequencies that then connect us to other energetic responses with the same frequency.

By sending loving thoughts to my coworker and aiming at healing our relationship, I was tapping into that potential within the Divine Matrix. What are you tapping into on a daily basis?

That was the process I went through in the beginning, fleshing out the idea over a number of years. Louise Hay talks about it all the time in her book, *You Can Heal Your Life*. She explains that by saying different affirmations, you are planting the seeds for different patterns, and then you'll reap different results.

I embraced the concept and saw minor results, but they were light experiences compared to the one I just shared on the walk, and meditating on the power and the idea that the Kingdom of Heaven is within us, so searching for it without just doesn't make sense. If we keep looking inside and exploring, then we will find that we can manage our thoughts, for example, and then we can control our lives in a way that can strongly affect our experiences. That is spectacular if you take time to really think and feel about it.

How It Works

When you understand deliberate creation, the practice of actively choosing to direct your thoughts, you will harness the immense power that is inside you to shift your experience of life. To direct our attention, we must first understand the nature of thought itself. At the most basic level, it's about frequency and vibration. If I am vibrating certain kinds of thoughts and feelings, I'll attract more of those thoughts and feelings, and more situations to experience those thoughts and feelings.

Consider the saying "misery loves company." There is actually a lot of truth in clichés that can bring a lot of wisdom to our lives. "Birds of a feather flock together" is another one. Certain kinds of people attract one another because they're vibrating at the same frequency. When you're feeling bad, what's the last thing you want to do? Be around someone who is super-happy. You just want to slap them upside the head and say, "Get away from me, you weirdo, because life sucks right now."

That's the Law of Attraction. Our past and present has led us to this moment of having certain thoughts and feelings. Just like right now, here, in this moment, you have attracted this book, this teaching about Gratitude, Appreciation, and Attraction.

What happens next is up to you. Will you allow this information to inspire you, depress you or be disinterested? It's actually ALL up to you. You can decide what you want this book or anything else in your life to be for you. Is it a tool or is it an obstacle?

Using our 'misery loves company' example, this person has the patterns of thinking unhappy things and rehashing how everything went wrong, how their life isn't good, how they wish it were different, and if everyone around them could just do and say different things, then everything would be alright.

When you allow these thoughts, you're giving your power away, and that is why you feel like crap. That's why we get depressed. Because when we get depressed, the idea is, "I have no control over my life. I am completely passive right now and there is nothing I can do to make my life better, so I am just going to stay pissed off, sad and depressed. Hand me that doughnut!"

I've been there and I can really relate to this. But it is the most limited point of view we can have on life. We can come out of this depression by taking simple actions. And it doesn't even have to be something as enlightened as meditating, prayer or reciting mantras and affirmations. We can watch a movie, decide to put a comedy on and when something strikes us as funny, be instantaneously lifted. Laughter is a great healer and so sometimes, even though we're depressed, we may somehow attract it in, because the Universe is always good on some level.

And then all of a sudden, there is Richard Pryor. I don't know how anybody can't laugh at that man. That man is just one of my favorite comedians ever. He just appealed to every type of audience out there, young, old, white, black, European, American. Everybody loved him and he knew a lot about what's true about life. We have all these funky perspectives for funky reasons and he pointed all these things out so we can start lifting ourselves up.

Once we start laughing a little bit, that is key. Because when we learn how to laugh at ourselves and laugh at our depression, laugh at our anger, we can think of ourselves as silly. Silly kids getting too caught up on life. If we take that lighthearted attitude, even if we get depressed, sad or angry, all of a sudden we have less of an attachment to it.

Once we start to lift ourselves up, all of the sudden the phone might start to ring because our vibration has started to lift and maybe someone who isn't ecstatically happy, but maybe something just a little bit good has just happened to them and they call and tell you. Maybe they say, "I just might be getting that job, so my life's not going to continue to completely suck." You are still attracting someone who might be somewhat negative, but maybe they have a little bit of a different perspective in that moment, and thus the Law of Attraction is always working.

As we start to raise our vibration, we start attracting different potentialities, so as we start to lift our spirits, we start to feel some different emotions within our chest, within our belly, within our being. All of the sudden, there is a different vibration, a different frequency being sent out. It's really like a radio. If you are looking for 98.7 but your dial is stuck on 102.7, you can't hear the music that is on 98.7. It just can't happen. We have to figure out how to adjust our frequency in our lives to receive what we want: the people, the opportunities, the jobs, the relationships, the experiences, the ideas, the philosophies.

Directing Our Attention

Before you can choose to think different thoughts, you must first become aware of the thoughts that currently exist in your mind. We all know people who are just drifting through life and have no desire or wish to become aware of themselves, or they think there's nothing wrong with what they're doing and yet a lot of the time, they are pretty unhappy people. They may not realize it, but ultimately, that is their choice.

It does not have to be that way for you. There is another way. It ALL starts with awareness. Awareness is one of the keys to making changes in our lives. There is something graceful and beautiful happening simply by becoming aware. It truly is a healing process in and of itself. I think that is why the Buddhist tradition has been such a powerful philosophy and religion throughout the world and so many people have turned to it, myself included, at troubled times.

Just becoming aware of ourselves, our bodies, our minds, our thoughts, our feelings, our patterns, our relationships... there are healing aspects to simply noticing them with an objective mind. As the Oracle said, "Know Thyself." When we know ourselves, we become aware of our bodies, our internal mental and emotional workings, our patterns, our beliefs systems, the different mental paradigms we carry around, the resentments, the joys, the depths of who we are. If we explore ourselves, there is a great deal of healing that happens without any gratitude, special exercises or anything else-- just that practice of simple awareness.

So where do we begin the process of awareness? Awareness of the breath, awareness of the mind, awareness of how the diaphragm moves up and down the body, awareness of the different sensations in the body, awareness of the senses, feeling the bottoms of our feet, are all great starting points. You'll find exercises later in this book which focus on awareness as a focal point to creating a very powerful connection within ourselves. That connection starts to spark up the circuitry, if you will, to be able to delve deeper to create significant change in our lives.

After you become aware of your thoughts, next you can practice directing them. The main key to it all is Practice, sometimes called 'The Mother of Skill'. For me, I thought that I had stopped thought, but the truth was I had been able to quiet the first few levels of noise, and that felt like stopping thought. It wasn't until years and thousands of hours of meditation later that I realized that what I thought two or three years ago was stopping thought, wasn't. I even questioned where I am now and where I was then, and did I really stop it then, or was I just going through this process of quieting my mind even more?

We don't realize the depth and breadth of our minds until we really commit to exploring it on an ongoing, consistent basis, in a daily practice. This daily practice becomes part of our life's journey, part of the beautiful tapestry that is 'us'. All of the practices and techniques for gratitude practice you'll learn in this book are wonderful, however, without a real daily practice, you won't see the results you would like to see. It doesn't have to happen 365 days a year, but I think it has to happen a minimum of 200 or so times a year for us to really make a significant change in our lives, where we look back and say, "Wow, I used to be this kind of person, and today I am this kind of person with much better opportunities, much larger potential and a much more beautiful life experience."

If we really want to have that kind of evolution within ourselves, then we have to dedicate ourselves to a daily practice. By a daily practice, I don't mean hours every day, but I do mean a minimum of 10 to 20 minutes a day, consistently over time, that's really going to have an effect. If we are very busy one day and we can only do the 2 minute exercise, that's fine. I've had a lot of days like that. And I've had a lot of days where I've done nothing. However, if we aren't careful, those missed days become months and years for some.

Is that what you want for your life? If not, I suggest learning how to set aside just the 10 to 20 minutes per day, every day. If we come back to it and we notice that, all of the sudden, we've strung together two or three days without any Gratitude practice, inner practices, any exploration or being aware of who we are, or what we are really feeling or thinking, we'll feel the difference. Say, "I've missed three days in a row now, I am going to do it right now, I am going to drop everything I am going to pull over to the side of the road. I am going to stop my excuses or whatever it is I am doing and just go do it. I am going to give myself that two minutes because I know that that two minutes is going to be the seed to feeling better and that will lead me to that 5 minutes, and that 5 minutes will help lead me to 20 minutes, and —so on until I can do this every week for 3 weeks straight."

When we build that momentum, it's like a wave that's just lifting us up day after day, practice after practice. Then, all of the sudden, we are at the top of that wave and we can see so much more from that height. If we keep practicing, that wave just keeps going up. When we stop practicing, that wave just curls over and we crash and splash. Riding that wave can be a tough practice, but it's good for us to crash and splash every once in a while, because then we get to see where we were and say, "Oh man, I really have to get myself back to together again. I've got to practice again." Daily practice is of the utmost importance. I have had the blessing of several teachers who have made that a very important point within my own practice.

After awareness and a commitment to consistent practice, you can explore various realms of deliberate thought. Visualization, prayer and meditation are three examples. For me, I do believe in a God, I do believe in a Source, The Force-- whatever you want to call it. I don't necessarily see it as a separate being and I don't see it as an old man with a long white beard sitting on a cloud. But I do believe that's the most powerful force in the Universe that actually informs everything else that is in the Universe and has that kind of seed within everything. That's what I think of as God. I think we are swimming in God right now, and that the Source is within us and without.

When I have that kind of belief, prayer becomes a very, very powerful practice for me because when I pray, I am speaking, communicating with all that is. If I have that belief, I am immediately lifted up and if I have the belief that visualization is really going to help me create the pattern or realize the path to what I want most in life, then that is going to be a very powerful practice. It is going to lift me up because I have that belief system supporting it. By belief system, I mean this construction of thought and belief patterns that comes together to create a paradigm, several different beliefs and thought forms that create a mental structure and intellectual apparatus. I think of Legos or Lincoln Logs, and all these thoughts are different pieces that we put together. The belief system becomes part of that, like a larger construction, and taking several of those belief structures together creates a paradigm.

A paradigm in our life is this large, intricate structure of how we live our life, depending on who we are with and what we are doing. We take on these different belief structures and we live our lives from and through these paradigms. Unless we take the time to truly get to know ourselves, in essence we are these paradigms and they drive our lives without us ever knowing what they are or where they are taking us.

A great practice of awareness is looking at how we act when we are with our buddies, when we are with our family, our co-workers, and when we are alone. What do we do, what do we think, when no one's watching? I get choked up just thinking about that because during our daily practice, we really get to see how we are different people in different situations. It helps us understand—whether we are using prayer, meditation, visualization, gratitude process— that they can be the tools we have in our toolbox to pull out when we need them, and if we get to the place where and when we are aware of what we need in that moment, then life just starts to become really smooth. Once you become aware of your thoughts, compassionately discipline yourself to the practice of monitoring your thoughts and implement them, you're ready to open yourself to how gratitude and appreciation can shift your internal and external life.

Chapter 2

Shift of Perspective

"Gratitude is not only the greatest of virtues, but the parent of all the others."

--Cicero

Before embarking on a practice of gratitude and appreciation, I want to address the very real question of what to do if you feel your life has nothing to be grateful for. In a prolonged period of pain and sadness, we become so accustomed to experiencing stress, unhappiness, confusion, depression, uncertainty and a lack of confidence, that we find it hard to alleviate ourselves from this state of *learned helplessness* and might prefer to remain there, rather than looking for techniques to remove ourselves from that state. Many people describe it as being on an emotional roller coaster. If you frequently watch the news and read the newspapers, you inevitably leave yourself exposed to dramatic, sad and even horrific stories. These accounts, after all, have, made the news, as they are not everyday occurrences and the media likes to dramatize the situation in order to grab our attention and sell commercial advertising against our attention.

You do, however, become de-sensitized and may become much more on edge without even noticing it. You may not notice it day-to-day, but what do you think happens to your mind, body and soul when you take in sounds and images that are disturbing to you? This kind of stress that is imperceptible to the untrained mind can lead to us to be particularly sensitive and to take things personally when it involves the important people in our lives—significant others, family, friends and co-workers. We begin to look at ourselves in a negative way based on their words, because they don't see us how we wish they would. They do not appreciate us the way we think they should, or at least they do not communicate in the way we wish they would.

There is, however, a different path available to us. If we don't take the time to appreciate our lives in a significant way, we may not realize there's an alternative option. Once we become aware of this, we can start to explore it. We have to explore this other option deeply—and not just for one minute or one day. You have to invest a few weeks at an absolute minimum, but I'd suggest a few months of testing it out.

Think about your life in terms of decades. The average person gets several decades. Therefore, if we live for seven, eight or nine decades, what's a few months to try something out that could potentially change our lives substantially for the better? If it doesn't work, you can give it up and move on, but what I've found for all the people who've invested time and effort in trying to appreciate their lives, they see an expansion that will last a lifetime.

Shift of Perspective

Consider the things and people you don't like and increase your awareness around your circumstances. Become aware of your attitudes and thoughts, and you'll come to learn that these patterns and the never-ending cycle of the ego, keeping us in a state of negativity, are really a result of the Law of Attraction. "As we think, so we receive. As we feel, so we receive." If our ego is feeling bruised and we can't believe people are putting us down or not responding to us or not loving us, that's a result of the message we're sending to the Universe.

It's imperative that we understand that we have a very powerful influence as divine human beings. That's called our "I Am" power and presence. As we repeat different things throughout our days and lives, there is an 'I Am' presence that then immediately gives you what you're referring to. It's like a genie that lives inside us, who will immediately give us what we say we're experiencing and what we focus on. All we do when we think about the negative aspects of our lives is build up an accumulation of more things we say we don't want. Every time we complain, act negatively, go into a depression, or get sad about things, our life acts as a mirror. We're just given more and more of the same.

If we feed the ego and allow it to direct our lives, we'll manifest ego-restricted situations. Just to be clear, the ego is a component that we actually need to live in human civilization and society, this individualized aspect of us. The "Hi, I am Matt" separation from personality that's really important when we're growing up in the world, because we do have individual physical bodies. The ego's job is to help us protect ourselves so we don't just leave our hands on a hot stove or walk in front of a truck. However, we may feed this ego over several decades with our thoughts of worry, stress, and negativity.

These three emotions amass and compound into that dumping ground for universal baggage and, as we continue to add to this pile of trash, we create a big magnet of negativity that, for the rest of our lives, just continues to attract more negativity. Yet, what is so amazing about this work is that once we make a change in our *energetic vortex,* our mindset, it is holographically sent to the many layers of our being—who we are and our whole lives.

Just because you may have been living a life of complaining, blaming or sadness etc., the moment you start to move in a more aligned direction, the Law of Attraction shifts and immediately starts to bring you more of the good energy that you are now channeling into your life.

The Big Three

If we look at the major situations in our life, such as our health, relationships and finances, we must be aware that it's in these areas that we experience the most resistance to change. How can we be grateful for our health when we're suffering from a medical challenge? How can we be happy in a relationship that's strained, abusive or even non-existent? How can we feel joy when we're struggling to make ends meet? If we find evidence of an unhappy life, a powerful reversal will happen when we take the time to strengthen our gratitude muscles.

Embarking on a practice of gratitude will start to protect us from life's harshness. It's like building a force field which allows us to thrive behind its protective barrier. This doesn't mean that we won't feel or be affected by what other people say or do, or what happens in the world beyond. A light is, however, built around us, through which everything has to pass, particularly our appreciation, making sure we live in gratitude. It filters out a lot of the brutality in our lives, which may previously have been, before our practice, a painful experience.

When we become more connected to ourselves through the practice of appreciation and the exercise of being grateful, it's a different lifestyle from taking things so personally and feeling each shot that life fires at us. We have something to turn to that allows us to feel the truth of our lives, which is that we have a tremendous, abundant amount of good things surrounding us. It comes down to our perspective and the simple truth is that we *always* have something to feel grateful about in our lives.

When you don't have a gratitude practice, when you aren't feeling appreciative about your life, you don't have that protection. You can't resort to that process that lifts you up above the noise and the fray and the confusion so that you can see things more clearly. That's really what gratitude and appreciation does—it lifts us up from all the earthly experiences that hold us down when we forget who we really are (divine children) and instead, turn our lives into negativity.

It takes us up and out of that and then we're able to see our lives more clearly, to see just how satisfying and fulfilling they really are. Think about what happens if someone doesn't like what we did. That's always going to happen, that's part of life, but if we take the time to emotionally invest in ourselves in a way that really brings up all those positive feelings of appreciation and thankfulness, feelings which lead to happiness and joy, then we have momentum building up and we don't have to allow their opinion of us affect our own opinion of ourselves. It's really hard to throw you off your roll if you're really connected to those good feelings constantly. That becomes the most powerful working energy in your life. The key to shifting to a gratitude stance is making things relative and accessible by focusing our attention on them.

In the case of health, this is a very simple practice that I've used for pain in the body and joints. If we have a painful left knee that is sore and tight, I focus on the right knee. I notice how well the right knee works. I feel glad and appreciative that my right knee works, compared to the left one. I can stand on it, swing it back and forth. I put my hand on it and I feel the genius of design that goes into my knee and think about how amazing this knee is, particularly with all the abuse I've put it through, and yet it still works so well and is so healthy! I meditate on how great my right knee is. You can of course use any part of your body. For example, if both your knees are sore, focus on your elbows or shoulders or some other body part.

Life is not just a mirror, it's a holographic experience. Whenever we focus on one aspect of ourselves that's 'good' or 'bad', that filters out and overflows into all the other areas of our life especially physically, if we're focused on something as concrete as our health. As we focus, that energy is increased. If we concentrate on how good something's working, how amazing it is, how grateful we are for it, then that energy transmits to other areas that aren't working so perfectly. If we focus on how bad the knee is and say "I am in so much pain because of my knee," that's my message to the Source, to the Force—whatever you want to call it. "I want more pain in my knee." That's the foundational message it's receiving. When it receives that message, it says, "Hmm, can I deteriorate that ligament a little more? Yes I can, sure, here you go!"

You see, we are extremely powerful and creative beings. We're effectively living in a world of clay and can just create whatever it is we want with our minds by the way we're thinking and feeling as we go through life. That is often a hard thing to comprehend when we're first being introduced to this idea, but as my wife can attest (boy was she challenged those first few years of our relationship!), she is also a believer now. Coming round to this way of thinking and understanding how much control we actually have was initially a difficulty for her. She told me, "Listen, I don't agree with all the things you believe."

I said, "You do what you gotta do, I'm just going to keep doing what I gotta do and we'll see what happens as we build our relationship."

I was in love with her and knew that I wasn't going to stop just because she had a different perspective on some things. Truth be told, I was completely confident that if I just kept living my life the way I lived it, she would see the positive results and experience it for herself. I didn't need to try to force her or teach her, or anything like that.

Different things would happen to me and she'd say, "Aren't you mad? Don't you want to yell at them or do something?"

My response was always, "No, I'm not going to do that, because I don't want more of a fight with that person."

"But they did this to you," she'd insist.

I decided that it was okay, it was their choice and I wasn't going to descend to their level. I don't want to dwell on the depravity of life, I want to live in and focus on its beauty! Why would I spend my time and energy focusing on the muck?

My wife thought I was crazy until the person in question would call me, reach out to me, apologize, do something great for me, or help me out in some way. She would be amazed at the change. Within a few days, radical transformations would sometimes occur involving someone who had previously done me 'wrong'. That's how it works, whether we're talking about health, our relationships or our finances.

With relationships, it is slightly trickier to understand how much control we have because the other person has their own free will. So we can't necessarily change specific people based on what we would like them to be. It is still possible to bring about change, but the other person has to be receptive to that kind of idea.

Here's the key—if we're vibrating goodness, beauty, infinite ideas, the feeling of being an eternal, magnificent being, I'm beautiful, I'm wealthy, I'm gorgeous, I am so loving and I am hot, then we're inevitably going to attract in people that see us in that way too.

Remember we're holographic, so once we allow that energy into our life, it filters throughout. Like water through a maze, it works its way through our life. If we increase the joy we feel, it blows any negativity out of the water. We won't even remember it any more. We obliterate it from our minds, because joy is an all-powerful kind of energy, this very fine spiritual energy. The negativity, the complaining, the wishing people were different all the time, the lack of acceptance and appreciation for the good things they do for us and with us, all succeed in leading us in the opposite direction than where we want to be.

I will therefore add a little disclaimer at this point, to the effect that if you're not completely ready or motivated to live your life in a much more joyful way that can bring positive changes, your experiences of all the wonderful things that life has to offer may be very limited. You do have to be careful with this practice, however, as this is powerful stuff. It will change your life quickly. It won't be something that takes a couple of years or more for things to change. No, it's going to change immediately, at the microscopic, quantum level, at the very same moment you change your perspective. Then, over time, it will compound and you will see it as you go through life in how people treat you, what they say, what they do for you. It's really amazing.

In respect of relationships, we all experience hiccups at times. This is totally normal, but when it comes to something like suffering emotional or physical abuse, I would never advise you to appreciate something you don't authentically appreciate. So if you really don't appreciate this person, we don't pretend that you're going to be grateful for him or her and then you'll be treated better. That's not authentic and not how this works.

If someone is very rarely emotionally abusive but at all other times they're this amazing human being, you can appreciate their positive aspects too. It doesn't mean you won't still question whether they're the right person. Any time we're being abused in any situation or relationship is an important time to question why we're there. I don't think we should ever say, "I'm not that good," or, "I only get abused every once in a while, so that's okay." Once we recognize that we're being severely taken for granted, whether it's in a physical or emotional way, or someone is trying to instill fear in us or manipulate us in what we perceive to be a scary evil way that creates stress and pain in our lives, it's time to really question why we're with this person and really question whether it is time to leave.

With that said there can be people who have volatile tempers, who yell, scream and completely lose it. God knows I've yelled and screamed at times, but I am aware that I did so out of stress, fear, confusion or a lack of understanding. I think we can forgive people and create opportunities although we still need to check to see if it's a safe place for us to be and if we really have what it takes to endure the process of potential change in this person.

If it's a pattern that's been going on for decades, chances are they ain't changin'! Lightning can strike and it does strike, but it's not something we can count on daily. We don't see lightning strikes in front of us every day. We see it every once in a while. In an abusive relationship, whether it's your boss, your boyfriend or your wife, that's a situation to really assess, become acutely aware of and decide what's really going on, and, if necessary, get the opinion of professionals or our closest advisors so that we can attempt to look at it as objectively as possible.

When it comes to money, I have a story that illustrates shifting your perspective through action. I found a penny that was heads up. I'll confide in you here that I pick up a penny whether it's heads up or not, but years ago, after spending time in a Buddhist temple, I was too embarrassed to pick up change and thought it was better to leave it for someone who needed it more than I did. It was fine, I'm glad I did that for a while. It was a wonderful feeling to know that I had left it for someone else, but this day, I picked it up because I wanted to try something new and channel as much abundance into my life as possible.

I also love to give away money, to donate to people. When they pump my gas, for example, I love to give them a few bucks. When I was out to eat out yesterday, the appropriate 20% amount to tip was $6 bucks, I gave $10. Not that it makes me Daddy Warbucks. But if I can afford that extra $4, why not make the server's day?

It comes back to that energetic kind of stamp, that energetic signature that we're sending out to the world all the time, whether it has to do with our health, our relationship or our monetary abundance, it's all the same. What we resonate, what we vibrate, whatever frequency we're tapped into, we're going to receive more of.

When I pick up that penny, I allow myself to feel like I've

just found a thousand dollar bill. That vibration is immediately working and I look for the interesting connections that result from being in that state. I gave my wife $100 cash a few days before I found the penny because she needed to give it towards a gift, which I was happy to give at the time. I found the penny the same day I gave the extra tip. I went home, happy with this shiny little penny in my pocket and as soon as I get in the door, my wife hands me $100. I asked what it was for, and she told me she didn't need the hundred dollars for the gift after all, we had apparently already paid for it.

It sounds simple enough. But within a short amount of time: tip, penny, I get $100. I notice the pattern because I spend time thinking about these things watching my life, and so can anyone else. Once you start to see these patterns, you'll be astounded at how cool they are! I ended up giving my wife that lucky penny.

All of this correlates with another law called the Law of Circulation. That's why I give the bucks to the gas station attendants. At weddings, I give a card and check, but for the people I'm close to, I like to take a $100 bill and slip it into the groom's pocket. You never know what things may come up during the wedding that the bride and groom may have to pay for.

That's the way I want to live my life. That's how I do it and it all comes back to me in spades. Much more than I've ever given out has come back to me—ten, fifty, a hundred times over. That's just the way this vortex of abundance works, flowing from a mountain of joy and gratitude that we build up. All of a sudden, our lives are just in the flow. Worry becomes a distant memory or when it does pop up, we allow ourselves to melt it away with awareness and joy. We turn our attention towards what's good in our lives; the simple abundant things like the roof over our head, the fact that we have a car that works, the fact that we have family members when some people have no family, the fact that we have a friend when some people feel all alone. We compare the good in our lives and see the opportunity to be appreciative of different things. Then we build up a huge focus and momentum on those aspects, which then become the power in our lives. They become that force field, that protection, that power that lifts us up by the seat of our lives makes us feel so much better about every single aspect of our world.

The key is to start where we're at. We can never start where we aren't. That's what being a physical being in a time-based life experience means. We start where we're at and immediately start creating new opportunities for ourselves, so even though we're in that down-and-out job making a meagre $4.50 an hour, it will occur to us to be grateful for that $4.50, for that penny dropped on the ground and grateful for the fact that we even have a job. We then become grateful for the buddy we have at that job.

You can become grateful you don't have to travel that far to get to that job. The hours are actually pretty good, even though you don't make as much money as you would like to. You start to turn your perspective on your relationship to that job and all of a sudden, you're going to get another offer. You'll see another job opportunity. The boss will come to you and say that it's time for your raise, that you're going to get $9 an hour—double your current pay rate. You don't know what it's going to be.

All the major spiritual disciplines of the planet have been talking about this for thousands of years. There's no mistake that in the Old Testament and the New Testaments, giving thanks is one of the most repeated aspects throughout. The reason why is that it's such a powerful principle. It's not being grateful for the things we don't like, it's being grateful for the things we do like, in spite of the appearances and experiences of the things we don't. It's a turning of the cheek, a turning of the mind, a changing of our perspective, rather than being thankful for what we don't like. Within the situations we don't like, we may think, "Sure, I make $4.50 an hour, but I get to stare at the ocean while I pick up trash on the beach." But if there's nothing redeeming about your job, be grateful that you have one and that will be the start to finding a new one that's a better fit for you.

The Little Things

So what we can do is establish a practice that leads to joy by appreciating the different things in our lives, by taking time every day, even if it's just for a few minutes to 'Count Our Blessings'.

Count the smallest things. What do we have? What's in the room with you right now that you can see and that you're grateful for. Even if you are blind and can't see your body, you can use your mind. Say that it's the middle of the night and you can't see anything, you can still remember this process. Is there any aspect of your body that's working nicely? Are you breathing? Do you sense warmth and cold? Do you have a roof over your head? Is your heart beating? Is your blood flowing? Are your organs doing their job without you having to remind them to do so? Even if it's a cardboard box, it's a roof that some people don't have.

I know it sounds radical but it's the truth. It's one of those things that, as we start to build up this new mountain of joy, then that ball of negativity connected to the ego really starts to melt. As it grows smaller and less powerful, less magnetic, the joy builds as we start to attract in more and more happy experiences—, things that we enjoy, things that we appreciate—into our lives. It's not that our lives become perfect all of sudden. We're always going to have resistance and contrast in our lives but that's not necessarily a bad thing, especially once we get a grasp of how to handle our own lives, because then we can see the contrast, negativity and all those things that we don't want as an opportunity to meet these situations with joy.

Then we will start to operate on a completely different level. We see the person stressed, confused, hurt and sad, and they're acting out while we are able to just relax our shoulders, take a deep breath, be grateful for what we've got and the opportunity that we get to meet this person with love.

I'll tell you, it just melts the other person. Not always immediately, but often they will see the look in your eye, they will feel the energy radiating from you, and they won't be able to refrain from acting a little bit softer, a little bit gentler, a little bit more thoughtful about what they're experiencing. It changes and creates so many more opportunities for us to experience the most beautiful things that life has to offer.

A great book that explains many of these aspects in detail is Gregg Braden's *Divine Matrix: Bridging Time, Space, Miracles and Belief*. As you read in this eloquently written piece below:

> *"Just as many artists refine an image until it's exactly right in their minds, in many respects it*

appears that through the Divine Matrix we do the same thing with our life experiences. Through our palette of beliefs, judgments, emotions and prayers, we find ourselves in relationships, jobs and situations of support and betrayal that play out with different individuals in various places. At the same time, these people and situations often feel hauntingly familiar. Both as individuals and together, we share our inner-life creations as a never ending cycle of moment layered upon moment, day after day, and so on."

What a beautiful, bizarre and powerful concept! Just the way a painter uses the same canvas over again while searching for the perfect expression of an idea, we may think of ourselves as perpetual artists, building a creation that's ever changing without end.

I really appreciate his artist analogy, as we are truly our painting our own lives moment to moment by how we are feeling and if we are feeling grateful and appreciative, which always feels WONDERFUL, guess what? That is the picture you are painting about your life and The Law of Attraction will just bring you more things to be happy about! What a system our Creator has put in place!

I truly believe that one of the most plausible explanations for why there is so much sadness, depression, anger etc. throughout the world is because we underestimate ourselves and the powerful creative power we have been given. Just like anything else in this life, with our focus, faith, and appreciation, we can bring about massive transformational experiences in our lives, which will make them irrevocably better than they ever were before.

People ask me, "So, you are saying all we have to do for all these great things to come into my life, is to be more grateful?" and the answer is a Divine, "YES!" I understand that this may be a huge mindset shift for some, however, just like I did, you can start small and build your way up over time. It's all part of an eternal process anyway.

Having a full toolbox of things you're appreciative of and living your life with gratitude acts as insulation from some of the stressful concerns of life. Therefore if someone cuts you off or says they don't like what you did or said, it somehow lessens the blow. Sometimes it dispels the effect completely, which I've experienced hundreds of times.

It really is something that can be shocking when it first happens. You hear something and you are aware that your old pattern from five, ten or twenty years ago would be to become offended that this person would say or do that, but now we have this new gratitude practice, our alternative response is, "Okay. I wish this situation was somehow different. I wish this person would act in a nicer way. However, I appreciate that it's really okay, I am fine, and I am just going to move on and let go." You don't let this incident bring you down because you have joy in your heart and you're going to stick with it, because Joy is Good!

Laughter and Comedy

Sometimes things are tough and can be sad and depressing. We've got to counteract that. A great way to do that is to find comedians that we like, actors and movies that we think are funny and inspiring, and people that make us laugh. I have a few friends who, every time I hang out with them, make it literally hard for me to breathe because I'm laughing so hard.

I love comedians. I always head straight for the comedy channels. I like older humor like that of Richard Pryor, Gene Wilder and their movies. We all have that person that just cracks us up—invite that into your life. Rent those movies, spend time reading those books that make you laugh, whether it's actual jokes or just looking at kittens and puppies playing on YouTube. Find the thing that brings real simple joy into your life that makes you laugh out loud. That is a beautiful, pure energy that is absolutely tremendous for our being to be bathed in.

There was a study done on smiling that I practiced just yesterday with my Mon and Dad. You just smile in the face of things you don't like. It feels rather fake and plastic at first but then you'll begin to laugh at yourself for even smiling during the situation All of a sudden, this huge burden is lifted from your heart. It's lessened by the humor, the smiling, the laughter.

There is a movement of laughter groups, where people simply get together and just laugh! There are also laughter yoga classes and the like. You're basically channeling joy and appreciation for something that's funny when we laugh, when we smile. There is a practice that you can carry out involving mirror work, where you do different things like looking into your own eyes and saying, "I love you, I appreciate you, I'm grateful for you, I approve of you, I accept you.", Make sure you smile at yourself!

This higher energy starts to seep in—this happiness, this joy. By not taking life so seriously, a heavy burden is lifted from our souls.

At that moment, just the ability to smile is something we can appreciate. I want to urge anyone who is reading this book or thinking of practicing this work to really invite in the simple joys of laughter, comedy and merely hanging out with friends or family who make us laugh. Then doing simple things like smiling at ourselves before we jump in the shower can make life easier.

I have found a great truth in my life that my Father, my Grandfather, and my beloved Aunt Rose have taught me, and that is the idea that more often than not simple is often better. Feeling good and better is rarely about more and so much more often about less. Even if it feels fake at first, try it for ten days in a row and watch what happens. I'm telling you, it works.

Chapter 3
Scientific Research

"Gratitude is the fairest blossom which springs from the soul."

--Henry Ward Beecher

We live in a society that often doesn't give credence to viewpoints unless there is sound scientific support in respected journals behind it. That being the case, I am very excited about the research surrounding the Positive Psychology movement and positive emotion, because it's proving what we've previously only surmised but have been told by mystics, spiritual teachers, philosophers and self-development teachers for thousands of years. As we focus our attention more on the positive emotions of contentment, appreciation, gratitude, joy, relaxation, fun and just being—letting go—our lives improve, and they improve significantly. Not only do that, they improve in a way that can be scientifically measured, offering hard evidence.

We're just on the cusp of this work; as a field of study, positive emotion is only about twenty-five years old, compared to the general study of psychology, which is closer to two hundred years old, and philosophy and religion, which are as old as civilization. We have therefore only scratched the surface of what may be possible through positive emotion research. But given the breakthroughs in this exciting field that have now begun to be publicized in the media, written about in books, discussed, debated and explored more deeply, I foresee more and more studies yielding further proof of how this kind of viewpoint can increase the quality of our lives as time goes on. I predict that in less than twenty years, positive emotions such as gratitude, appreciation, joy, and possibly even radical practices such as self-love, will be seen as very important not only to emotional health, but physical health as well. They may even be taught as topics in high school health classes, but first, especially in the USA, we need to stop relying on pharmaceuticals to change our thought processes. Anyone who's explored this in any detail will know the averages bear out and that the long-term effect of pharmaceutical drugs to help emotions is really terrible for you. Now, of course, there are many cases where someone has a chemical imbalance or similar and one should always consult their health professional before coming off such drugs.

Furthermore, if you're not in some seriously clinical depressive state, it's important to stay away from these substances. We call them pharmaceuticals, medication, mind-altering drugs, prescription drugs, over-the-counter, under-the-counter, behind-the-counter drugs—whatever you want to call them, at the end of the day, they're messing about with the chemicals in our brain.

As books such as *Prozac Nation* discuss, these drugs can actually make your life much worse. The science is showing that we can change the chemicals in our brains just by changing the focus of our attention and by investing time concentrating on alternative thoughts. Nature has its own way of healing us and when we learn just how to apply its remedies, we will probably not need to see a doctor again for a long while, let alone have to buy expensive medications from a pharmacy.

If we can do that from inside and access the Divine Medicine Chest that is within us, why would we want to use some outside thing with additives or side effects we aren't aware of? It's shocking just listening to those commercials about pharmaceuticals, some of which contain fifteen or more terrible side effects. These effects could jeopardize our wellbeing instead of making us feel better mentally. You could pass out, die, swell up like a tomato—all these things could happen to you, yet they keep showing all these smiling people on screen, happily encouraging you to buy these potential poisons.

These commercials should be illegal because they're portraying something that is not true, and yet there are billions of dollars behind them. So I'm putting myself behind the Positive Psychology movement, hoping that the more this information gets out there, the more people will choose to go within themselves rather than outside for relief, and therefore have a more harmonious path to fulfillment, health and healing.

I truly believe that in the next two or three decades, there will be tens of millions of people on this planet practicing gratitude, appreciation, massage therapy, meditation, receiving acupuncture, and doing yoga, tai chi, and chi kung. There is just too much scientific evidence that these non-invasive, non-chemical techniques raise our vibrations, increase our health, heal diseases and help us to feel good in the short and long term. This movement has already been going on for many decades and will continue to grow, evolve and develop.

Just look around your local town. There used to be one doctor, one hospital, no massage and no yoga. Now, there are dozens of places to help you feel better and get healthier in every single town. In larger cities, there are hundreds of choices, reinforcing that this trend is here to stay.

I know that gratitude, appreciation and positive psychology go hand-in-hand with this movement. Over the next century, I can see the average life span increasing to 120 or 130 years, with many of the elderly feeling the way active seniors do now in their late seventies and eighties. With natural medicines and technology, there's no reason why that would not be possible. Maybe we could even get there in fifty years!

Showing the scientifically tested evidence for gratitude gives the logical mind something with which to connect. In a way, using science to support something that is really more emotional, spiritual and psychological is like working behind the back of the ego. Now we have 'real' information, we've got 'proof' and the ego loves proof. If we can get the ego on board with our goals to develop ourselves emotionally, we remove a tremendous resistance point; we become real believers, we have faith, we know it to be true. Once we become real believers and are living from deep faith, there are no limits.

This chapter mentions just a sampling of studies on the effects of gratitude and appreciation but I'll let the research speak for itself! Please see the upcoming follow up to this book on mattogradycoaching.com for interesting studies that empirically show the beneficial effects of practicing gratitude.

Researchers have found that we have a happiness "set point," meaning that we may experience spikes or valleys in our lives, but after a time we generally revert to roughly the same level of happiness. Depending on your outlook, it may be uplifting or depressing to think that, regardless of events either horrific or wonderful, that you'll go back to feeling the same way you did beforehand. The great news is, though, that we are able to raise our happiness set point through gratitude and appreciation (Emmons & McCullough (2003).

Emmons conducted an experiment wherein he split his subjects into three groups. One group was told to make a weekly list of five things for which they were grateful, over a period of ten weeks.

This 'gratitude group' was compared to another group who was asked to track the hassles of their week, as well as a control group which simply listed the events of their week without labeling them as positive or negative. The groups kept journals of their moods and happiness levels in the weeks preceding the study to form a baseline measurement. The study revealed that the gratitude group felt a full twenty-five percent (25%!) happier after the ten-week study, compared to those in the control group and the hassle group. This is a huge improvement—tremendous! If someone came up to you and said practicing this technique for 3 weeks would make you twenty-five percent happier, would you do it? I sure hope so! I definitely would.

Gratitude is one of the simplest, easiest, most enlightening opportunities available to humankind. Studies like this provide measurable results, allowing you to replicate the conditions of the study if you're skeptical, so that you can see the results for yourself.

The grateful group didn't only see an increase in happiness, they also reported increases in alertness, enthusiasm, determination, attentiveness and energy; they were also more likely to report having helped someone with a personal problem or having offered emotional support to another person. Essentially, this evidence supports the theory that the more grateful you are, the more generous and more loving you become, not to mention happier, more enthused about life, more focused and energized—who wouldn't want that?!

Gratitude can be the path to all the other things you want in life! Appreciating life seems just too simple an act to be so powerful but just because something is simple does not mean it lacks power.

Often the exact opposite is true. How simple does breathing seem? We don't need to think about it, yet what would life be without it? Really short, for one! Thankfulness can work the same way in our lives: the more we focus on it, the more it grows and the more opportunities open up for us to be grateful. Life is not just about feeling good, but the feeling sure does help us to be catalysts for others to feel good around us.

Have you ever known a person who had a genuine happiness about them? People who walk into a room and everyone just feels better the moment they arrive? You can be that person, or maybe you already are. That person, I am sure, is grateful, happy in their own skin, appreciates what life has to give them and expects more good to come. They often have a quiet, knowing smile and perform random acts of kindness that don't always make immediate sense. These are the people I love to be around and the kind of person I aim to be every day. Who do you want be?

Better Quality of Sleep and Coping

In another study, this time conducted by Wood et al. (2009), it was revealed that people who thought grateful thoughts experienced a better quality of sleep than those who did not. Through a series of questionnaires, their participants reported greater sleep quality and duration, and less daytime dysfunction compared with those who did not practice grateful thoughts. This is such great news for any of us who have trouble falling asleep or wake during the night due to stress and worry. The study's results show that those who thought grateful thoughts were less likely overall to be negative or to worry, and were more likely to think positively. Therefore, gratitude can increase the quality of sleep and our basic coping skills.

Developing our coping skills is an important aspect of how we deal with stress. If we can reduce the stress in our lives and find ways to lessen its effects on our health and mindset, how much would it improve the quality of our lives? I have personally seen a tremendous shift in my own life and the lives of people I have worked with on this subject. There is a growing body of research that suggests stress, anxiety and worry are the mental states which set the stage for the most damage to the body and mind.

If you are in a grateful state, you are unable to be in a stressful state—you just feel too good! Thankfulness takes your mind and heart in a completely different direction. There are millions of sleep sufferers across the world. How much better could their lives be if they took just a few minutes each day to simply practice gratitude and appreciation? How much more rest would they receive?

We heal as we sleep at our deepest levels. Full, healthful sleep allows our bodies to move towards homeostasis, reducing how hard the body has to work to detoxify, fight cancer cells and so forth. Sleep ensures that we're doing all we can to attain our optimal health levels, so if gratitude can help, it's certainly worth a try.

Furthermore, the thoughts we have immediately before we drift off to sleep are very important. These are the images, ideas and thoughts we bring with us during our time in the unconscious state. It's important to plant the seeds of what you want more of in your life just before going to sleep. Even if it's just for two minutes every night before I go to sleep, I read something spiritual, inspired, or relaxing and I have noticed a huge, positive difference in my sleep patterns since instituting this practice.

In a study focusing on the effects of Positive Psychology, Martin Seligman et al. conducted a series of exercises on five groups and measured the effects on the participants' emotional states, both immediately following the experiment as well as over time. Three of the interventions greatly increased the participants' happiness and decreased negative symptoms.

The most interesting were the 'Gratitude Visit' and 'Three Good Things', similar to the journal-keeping exercise in the Emmons study mentioned earlier. For the gratitude visit, participants wrote a letter of gratitude to someone, made an appointment with the person they wanted to thank and then read it aloud in their presence. Participants in this group reported a substantial increase in happiness when reviewed by the researchers one week later.

Participants in the Three Good Things journaling group reported significantly higher levels of happiness and lower levels of depression than the control group, not only a week later at the follow-up interview, but at three- and six-month reviews with researchers as well. Despite not being instructed to do so, it was found that participants who voluntarily continued the gratitude practices were more likely to keep experiencing the benefits. The researchers concluded that there are multiple methods of lastingly increasing happiness and decreasing depressive symptoms, not just one!

This is scientific evidence and not mumbo-jumbo. This is real proof that positive practices like gratitude, forgiveness, joyful living and active loving help us to have better lives, long term! The fact that these practices are scientifically proven to help people who have symptoms of depression is simply amazing. The results did not feature on the front page of the New York Times nor run as a special headline on CNN, but that doesn't make it any less true. It just means that it may not have been dramatic enough to make the news—yet.

The effects of positive psychology will soon be impossible to ignore. In my opinion, most cases of unhappiness and stress may not need drugs or traditional therapy to improve. What we need is more appreciation, gratitude, thankfulness, joy and love in our lives. Now, that is a prescription *I* would sign up for!

Depression plagues millions of people worldwide. What could our society be like if people slept better and felt less stressed, were happier, more loving and more grateful every day for what they had? I can imagine its beauty, and to me it sounds like Heaven on Earth.

In order to work out why these positive states work for us, it is necessary to take all the information into consideration. The participants in these research studies were not forced into the research; they volunteered. Often though, these people are not informed exactly what's being tested. Researchers try different tactics to get reliable information from them because whenever people are communicating about how they feel, their thoughts can be amorphous and offered in an unstructured way.

One major factor of the experiments that will help you be as successful or more than the subjects is commitment. We see in the studies that the people were willing to commit to the process. They're being tested over weeks and sometimes months. As we commit to a process in our own lives, it's a similar proposition. Sure, those participants may have a scientist or psychologist asking them questions, as opposed to us asking the questions of ourselves, or a coach or a therapist or whoever it is we choose to work with, but the key is that commitment is crucial in order to stick with the process; to have the resolve to consistently turn our attention to something we haven't previously examined.

My experience is that we don't often need years of gratitude practice to see an improvement in our lives. Often, I see improvement after just a few sessions if the student is practicing on a regular or daily basis. Remember this work does not need hours. We are literally talking about five to ten minutes per day to start seeing profound effects. A few minutes in the morning and a few minutes at night can truly be enough to transform our lives.

Whenever we introduce something new like this into our lives, we can't just try it for one weekend and then say it worked or didn't work. We need, at a minimum, several weeks of practice. I advise all of my clients to give it at least two or three months, because it's subjective. For some people it happens in three seconds, the moment they focus on gratitude. For others, it may take longer. In my case, the change came quite fast. When I started this gratitude process, I was in a tough state of mind: depressed, sad and confused. I said, "What the hell? I have nothing to lose, I'm already pretty depressed and pissed off." I was very surprised that it actually worked for me and even more surprised at the speed.

Seeing how swiftly this process worked in my own life is one of the reasons I am so passionate about it and believe so deeply in it. When I think of people who are deeply depressed or sad, logical thinking says it's going to take a long time; it's going to be really hard to get to the point where they're feeling better.

That, however, was not the case for me. It was almost instantaneous; not that it didn't happen in stages, because it certainly did, but feeling that little bit better, when you're that low, is near-miraculous.

Look at being stuck low on the emotional scale, feeling really sad, doubtful, feeling that all is lost. You're not sure if you'll ever be able to climb out of that hole. Imagine how any sort of improvement at all can seem like a beacon of shining light. That's how I saw it, and it lifted me up and out of that hole within days. It started as simply noticing a difference in my emotions, although I wasn't really sure.

As the hours went by, I'd switch back and forth from being very low and depressed to curious about why I was suddenly feeling better. In a span of a few days, I was feeling better consistently, a feeling which lasted for hours at a time. That led to feeling even better. Within three weeks, I was completely out of the hole and felt no reason at all to go back in. That sad, depressive pattern had been broken.

It was many years before I ever got melancholy or deeply sad again and I certainly never went back to the desperately low place I had been when I got out of the Navy. I didn't go there again, even when, about ten years later, I experienced another sad time. Instead of returning to my previously depressive state, I employed the same gratitude technique I'd learned before, and it worked like a charm. That's why I'm so inspired to share this information with people, because not only did it help me once, it changed my life twice.

The best news of all is that you don't have to have a PhD or be a researcher to recreate the results of the experiments I've discussed in this chapter. A simple way of adopting the scientific methods I've seen work in my life and with my clients is by keeping a journal. Be sure to note what you're feeling and what's happening for you, what kinds of emotions you're experiencing, your state of mind. Record the date and some details of what's going on.

Over time, you'll be able to look back as you practice appreciation, as you increase your focus on what you're grateful for in your life. A sense of thankfulness will move through you on a daily basis. You'll be able to look back on these times and track your progress; to be a scientist in your own right, focused on the laboratory that is your mind and your heart. This laboratory is the place where we can make significant advancements in our own research on ourselves. At the end of the day, isn't that what matters most?

"Know thyself," the great teachers from ancient to recent times tell us; why not listen? Researchers establish a baseline based on the average person, what they're communicating and what's happening. They then introduce different techniques and exercises, measuring the results over a period of time and noting and categorizing any changes. A journal allows you to establish your baseline, much like in the experiments. In your own gratitude experiment, don't compare yourself to anyone else. This is like enrolling at a gym and turning up on the first day, only to find all those around you with biceps like Arnold Schwarzenegger, or being a slightly overweight female hoping to lose weight and only seeing perfectly-formed, flat-stomached models grinning back at her from the magazine she's reading.

As I tell my clients: Compare and Despair! Instead, use your journal to determine whether YOU have increased in happiness or lessened depression. In any sort of self-developmental spiritual process, that's what we need to focus on. Where we were, where we are now and where we want to go. As soon as we go outside ourselves and start comparing, that's when we have issues. Am I ever going to be as spiritual or as advanced a human being as Jesus, as intelligent as Leonardo DaVinci or as compassionate as Mother Teresa? Probably not. That doesn't mean that I can't aim to be spiritual, by expanding my mind and being kindhearted and compassionate. I look at where I was and then look at where I am today and see significant improvement and I am proud and happy with where my journey has taken me.

That's the real key. If we're improving our own lives, then we're succeeding. Even if we aren't improving, if we have the perspective to say overall, "I'm working on this, I can get there," then it's possible. Because we all step back and assess our lives at different points in time: the dawn of the New Year, weddings, births, deaths and other milestones.

One thing I've noticed, which is very helpful, is that with any step back, there is an opportunity to take a quantum leap forward! So as we see ourselves falling back into old patterns or habits, say the affirmation, "I'm stepping back so that I can leap forward." It opens the window to trusting the process and realizing it's a long journey, with many twists and turns, valleys and mountain tops, deserts and oceans.

Learning to adapt and be in the flow of our own journey is one of the many keys to living a happy life. Yes, we live moment-to-moment, so when we have a tough day or hit a rough patch, all we need to do is keep the faith. As the old adage goes, "This, too, shall pass." It's an overall process that we've invited into our lives, and for it to unfold as it needs to, based on all our life experiences and all the factors that go into any sort of gratitude-building, self-developing, spiritual, heart-opening experience, we need to trust it. Simple tasks like keeping a journal allow us to go back and really study ourselves and our lives, which can do wonders to help keep us in an enjoyable state.

As we know, life goes by too quickly. The river of life is always moving, flowing, changing. If we don't step in and go with the flow, it can disappear underneath our feet like sand while we're standing in the ocean waves. Similarly, the past can seem to disappear quickly in the background and the hard-won progress we've made over time seems insignificant or outside our control. Your journal can be the tracking device of the scientific experience that happens inside us once we adopt a real practice of gratitude, peace, contentment and joy in our lives.

Chapter 4
Exercises

"As we express our gratitude, we must never forget that the highest appreciation is not to utter words, but to live by them."

-- John F. Kennedy

This chapter contains a number of exercises you can use to bring the practice of gratitude into your life. Whether you've got an hour to devote or if you're pressed for time, whether you want to incorporate gratitude as you move through the activities of your day or whether you're challenged to come up with something to be grateful for, you will find something here for you.

A Time to be Grateful:
Exercises for Your Self

Breathing Exercise
The Breath—what is life without it? Often for the human mind, the only way we can really feel and appreciate something is when we consider what life would be without this 'thing.' As the saying goes, "we take most things for granted until they are gone."

However, that does not have to be your experience. You can choose to become grateful now! Try a quick exercise for me: think of your most favorite person in the world, spouse, parent, child or friend. Think about their relationship to you and how much they mean to you. Think about how grateful you are for them being in your life, picture their face smiling at you.

Now, picture them gone. Moved away, dead, gone. How do you feel? Trust me when I tell you that The Breath is like that favorite person of yours; it's your child, it's your best friend, your lover.

Now, go back to thinking about what life would be like without air. Picture life, with ten percent less oxygen, picture life with twenty-five percent less, at that point we would move like sloths, and who knows how long we would be able to survive. Hours? A few days? The Breath is your ally, your savior, your life giver. Doesn't it make good sense to pay some attention to it? It brings in the oxygen into our bodies, which goes into our blood stream which then fuels and transports all of what we need to survive to all the ready and waiting cells...

Can you see the painting I'm working on here? Since it's absolutely necessary for the continuation of human life on this planet, I hope you won't tell me that 'reality show' you watch every night is more important than spending some time paying attention to how the breath moves into and out of your body, providing you life? Not to mention there is a whole separate opportunity that is available once you become truly intimate with The Breath.

If you are interested in feeling, experiencing and being more abundant and prosperous in your life, coming into a conscious awareness of The Breath can do just that. How? Well, I'm going to tell you! Being that The Breath is so important to keeping us alive, as we begin to explore The Breath moving in and out of us, fueling us, giving us life with each breath, one begins to see, feel, and experience how The Great Mother feeds us. In this act, in this conscious acceptance and awareness of what is occurring as we breathe, we are abundant and prosperous, and through the Law of Attraction, bringing more of it into our lives.

Breath is also how Spirit is constantly moving through us. It's not just a physical act, there is also another act that we are still scientifically unaware of and yet, that is still a fact for anyone who has experienced it: The Breath is a Spiritual substance. As we explore the depths of The Breath, moving into, through us with our minds and open grateful hearts, we are aligning ourselves with its Beauty, with its power.

Try this now: Sit straight in a chair, crown chakra picking up your head, slowly, gently and gracefully open your chest, shining your heart to the world that loves you. Feel the weight of your body in the chair, grounding you, gravity cradling you. Feel your skin where it's being touched by the chair, your clothes, or where the air is touching your skin. Notice the temperature of it as it brushed your skin.

Now bring your awareness to The Breath, just watching, not adjusting anything about your cadence. This is not Breath work, this is Breath Awareness Practice. Allow yourself to belly breathe, like a baby. Don't hold your stomach muscles in, rather, allow them to move and your diaphragm to flow up and down in your chest and torso cavity. By now, because of the Power of Attention, I am sure your breath has changed.

See? You don't need to do anything, but allow the Awareness, the Intuition of the Body and the Soul to work with one another and have your ego sit this one out! Staying connected to the Ground and Gravity, relax as The Breath continues to undulate through your body, notice where it enters and exits your body and imagine it with your mind's eye traveling into your lungs, and how the energy moves down past your lungs and into your organs.

What is that? Is that your diaphragm? Yes, but it's more than that, that is Spirit bathing you in its light, in its Beauty. Accept this blessing, but continue to direct your attention to the process, to the continuous, ongoing experience of it. Allow your mind to ride it in and out, in and out and do this for at least five minutes.

Once you have spent some time just watching, and allowing, begin to notice if you have any natural gratitude for this process, for this knowledge, experience, for The Life-Giving Breath itself. Feel that gratitude deep down in the bones of your soul. Know this gratitude, and practice this when you feel a need to reconnect, recharge, or be grateful, or just as part of your daily appreciation process.

Grounding Exercise
My best grounding technique is using the body and the senses to connect deeply with your human form, to truly inhabit our beautiful temples; becoming aware of the Law of Gravity on our bodies, feeling the sense of gravity, connecting with our surroundings in a conscious way.

Start by getting comfy in a chair, feet flat on floor, body at right angles, feeling the WEIGHT of gravity on the body. Relax, eyes open. Notice where body touches the ground, the chair, etc. Really feel that weight, the connection with the physical, the earth. Begin to sense the bottoms of the feet, where our grounding energy comes from. Notice sensations, tingles, etc.

Use your attention to bring the focus up the body from the feet, feeling the skin, the bones, the blood, the veins, the cells of your body, you are filling your body with consciousness, with love. Come up your legs, into the shins, knees and thighs, rest here. Feel the whole of your legs, one at a time if it's not easy to focus on both....feeling the skin but also inside your body, staying connected to the weight of your body. Keeping eyes open so you don't go into a trance and get pulled away from the body, relax the whole body, release any tension.

Move your focus up the body into the hips, sacrum and pelvis, feeling all the parts, loving all of yourself deeply. Gently using your mind to connect and love your body. Notice connections of skin to clothes, chair, etc. Feel the weight in your bum connected to the chair.

Keep coming up slowly, gently with your mind's eye on your stomach, lower back, pause here, connect with your organs, picture them moving and working harmoniously in your body, bringing healing and nourishment.

Move up into the chest and upper back, connect with your heart, your lungs, your diaphragm as it moves up and down with your breath, the air that keeps you alive. Breathe deeply and gently here, feel the air, become grateful for your beautiful heart that you love with, where you receive love from the Universe, your fiancé(e), your children, your friends, awaken to its healing powers. Love your SELF! Breathe into any tension. Relax and let go, trust. Releasing any tension that arises or that you become aware of.

Staying connected in the body, go into your shoulders, noticing the presence in your whole torso, and legs, the feet connected, grounded to the earth. Direct this present energy down into your arms, feeling it flow, with your mind's eye. Filling your limbs with life, beauty, usefulness. Come up into the throat and neck, release, relax. Appreciate your communication powers of voice, all the beauty you have spoken.

Move your neck gently, release your shoulders. Move up into your head, your amazing brain, your eyes, your ears, your nose, your mouth, your lips. Relax your jaw. Sense it all, feel the tingles, the sensations of your beautiful face. Feel your WHOLE BODY at once. Connected, Grounded, Alive. Notice what you can see, don't move your gaze, just gently take in the impressions and be grateful for the ability to see. Go through all your senses the same way, experiencing them as you move through one by one, knowing you are alive, in body, loving your human form. To the ears and hearing, sounds that are close and sounds that are far away, simply listening, tasting, notice what you can taste in your mouth, on your tongue, feel your gums, your teeth, smelling, notice any aromas available, sensation in the skin--feel the whole organ of your skin.

The Grateful Day:
Opportunities and Releasing Resistance

Awakening Exercise

The first awakening moments in the morning are ripe and fertile with opportunity. The first direction we take our minds in sets the tone for our experiences throughout the day. Don't allow momentum, society or anyone else to decide what direction your day is going to go in.

I create a statement, affirmation, saying or prayer to shape my day. I start off with something simple like, "I am a magnificent divine being. I am of the divine spark, simultaneously acknowledging who I am and from whence I have come—God, the Source, the Force, the Universe." So just in the first two words, I've established a strong connection and the direction I want to go in. It takes all of three seconds to cultivate this fertile ground.

I start to focus on what I'm grateful for. I'm cozy and warm in a comfortable bed. No matter how my sleep was, right now I am thankful. It's really a game—anything of something is more than nothing of it. Any money we have, any food, any roof, any friend, any support is better than having none.

We're now able to move forward knowing what we do want. You may not be where you want to be in life as you're reading this book, but knowing and appreciating where you are can help you eventually get where you want to be. Your physical body is protected if you have shelter.

I bring my feet to the floor and connect with my slippers, the rug, the hardwood floor. Then I'm grateful there's a floor there. This may sound ridiculous, but not everyone has a floor—some people have dirt, a reed mat, a tent. This exercise is about simplifying our point of view, slowing down our lives to allow us to appreciate just what we *do* have.

As I get out of bed and walk across the room, I'm thankful for that ability. Walking is one of the most important, divine gifts that exist. Jesus talks so much in the Four Gospels about how they walked. Of course, they didn't have cars, but he could just have said 'they went'. Walking is like the perfect motion, it charges our bodies in the way it gently massages our organs as we swing our arms. Even if your perspective is from a wheelchair, you can do this exercise.

In the past I was not been able to walk, I've been on crutches, in leg braces, I know what it's like to be in pain and not able to move easily. If we're able to move at all, it's more than what some people can say. Evacuating our bladders and bowels, being able to brush our teeth and drink a glass of fresh, clean water are opportunities for gratitude. I have food in the fridge, I have delicious eggs, I have a kitchen. There are so many without. Why not be grateful for all you do have?

Then into work—I'm grateful that I have an office, a computer, amazing technology that allows me to run my business and help other businesses. Even social media. Technology is the most important thing for entrepreneurs and so much is free, like Gmail and Facebook. I have a cell phone, landline, I can call and connect with people. The one difference we need to have to be able to notice these things is that at each point, it's a certain perspective I'm choosing to have. I could look on the negative side and instead of saying, "I have this warm cozy bed that allows me to sleep," I could say, "I've only got a King-sized bed, I would rather have a California King," or, "I wish I had gotten that other pillow-top, it was only a couple hundred more." Instead of complaining, we can choose a different way of looking at things. Sometimes it's okay, because it sparks us to make other choices. "I would like to have one someday soon."

Even take note of the weather; if it's something you don't like, such as rain, notice it as something good for the planet, the water supply will end those droughts and give people the valuable water they need to drink and bathe in, it's an opportunity to move a little slower.

Waking up this way sets a pattern of taking the highest perspective in that moment available to us and applying that to our day. It sets ourselves up for the next moment to do the same thing and the next and so on, so we can perpetuate all the goodness we are experiencing for as long as possible. Some of my clients are experiencing all of this for the first time, sometimes they just cannot believe how good they feel, they are shocked that good feelings can last for hours, even days if you really go deep. I ask you, why wouldn't you want this experience?

Cleansing Your Body Exercise

One thing that has been lost on our society is that cleansing ourselves and our bodies is a sacred practice. For most of my life, brushing my teeth, cutting my nails, taking a shower and washing my hands were things I had to get done as quickly as possible so I could get down to what I really wanted to do. When I was in the US Navy, I often had no choice but to shower in a minute or less, which, of course, you are happy to do when the water is cold! For many years now, as I started some inner-cleansing practices, there has always been this nagging thought that there was something more available through this process. As I meditated on it, it started to unfold in my mind that anytime we cleanse something on our bodies, our hands, our feet, our faces (hopefully not in that order!), it is an opportunity to connect with ourselves on a very deep and powerful level.

Our bodies are our connection, the intermediary, the 'Bridge', if you will, from our Soul to the world. Attention to it, care of it and cleansing of it are of the utmost importance. This process needs to be done with loving acceptance and open awareness. The body has messages for us if we have the ears to listen to our organs, our hearts, our genitals and reproductive areas, down to our eyelashes. I adopted this practice several years ago and it continues to grow and expand in ways I never thought possible.

Here's a way to use it when you're out and about. There are times when I am out at a restaurant with a friend and after using the bathroom, I approach the sink with a renewed awareness as I begin to connect with my Self, see my face in the mirror, look into my own eyes and send some love to my Self from my Self. I am grateful for the bathroom, for the restaurant, for my friend and, as I begin to wash my hands, I train my body and my mind to have a laser-like focus on this process. I feel the coolness as I touch the faucet, sensing its inner workings as I turn the knob, connecting to the ground, feeling my feet on the floor, having my concentration deep into my body rooted and grounded into the earth. I remember that I am a Divine Soul, having a human experience that is full of gratitude, remembering the Life Giving Breath and the fact that I am performing a sacred act of cleansing my Self.

As the water hits my hands, it sends a gentle shiver down my spine, my nerves are alive and kicking, my skin becomes aroused and awake. I adjust the water temperature to a hot that is not burning and then find the soap. I press down on the dispenser, actually feeling the soap ooze and push out through the spout as if it's another appendage I have acquired.

My sense of smell and texture become alive, as I feel and smell the soap the instant it touches my skin. Then the act of bringing my two God-given hands, wet with warm water, together with this blessed citrus soap in between them, I am often in a full state of ecstasy right there and then!

As I start to slowly and firmly rub my hands together, the smell pushes up towards my face. I watch the bubbles and feel as if I am a witness to creation itself. I watch the flow of the water. It often has a subtle beauty that is all its own. I rub the soap all the way up to my wrists, washing them as if it's the first and last time, all at once. I notice the shape of my hand, its different contours, the delicious sensations of heat, wet, and slipperiness. Watch how effortlessly they move in concert with one another to get the job done, noticing even the details of my hand and fingerprints as they slide over one another, all the while doing this with a relaxed belly, shoulders, jaw, neck, etc.

Then I wash my hands clean of soap with warm water so there is no soap left. I turn the water on cold. It's such a delightful transition and gives my divine body a little thrill as I then turn my hands up in a cupping motion, bring my face to my hands and splash this awakening, cold water to my face. I feel the aliveness in my Soul, the appreciation for such divine gifts in a final act of connection with the Truth.

Then I consciously dry my hands, hopefully in an air dryer, and then I float back out to the table, ready for whatever may come next in my blessed life.

Making Love Exercise

Okay, what's not to be grateful for, right? I have a theory about having sex and making love, and that one of the reasons humans enjoy it so much more than other species, is because it truly brings us into the moment and gives us access to some of the higher, more beautiful aspects of who we are. We aren't thinking about the past or worried about the future in these moments. We are focused in the moment and we really give our spirit the opportunity to flow. It just doesn't get much better than that.

'Making Love' is really about allowing beauty, best feelings to which we have access, to enter into our lives as we spend time with another human physically. It's about allowing our hearts to expand with enjoyment as we are with our lover.

The Body becomes the medium in which we experience this process; being aware of our bodies, connected to our hearts, and sensing every brush, every stroke, every sensation in our lips as we kiss, allowing ourselves to be lifted up by the experience, yet not lose ourselves completely. Listening with our body to our partner and aiming at becoming as One with them.

If you are feeling adventurous, you can attempt to align your breath with your partner's and watch how that connects you even more deeply. We are sending and receiving messages throughout the experience that allows us to enjoy the moment as fully as possible while staying conscious and aware of our appreciation of the experience.

When we significantly move into this space, we can 'make love with life', and this is not physically about sex. It's about approaching life in the moment, letting go of the past, not looking to the future, just being with beauty that is now, in this moment. Focusing our attention lovingly on whatever is in front of us. What can you see that is beautiful in this moment? What feels good in this moment? Bring love to it. Listen to it. Become One with it.

Note: If this exercise interests you, be sure to check out David Deida's work in Tantra.

I Don't Want to Be Grateful:
Exercises for when you think you have nothing to be grateful for

Personal Gratitude Exercise

Who are you most grateful for in your life? If it's hard to pick someone, just go with the first person that comes to your mind. This can be a family member, friend, lover, spouse, coach, teacher or anyone else. Once you have someone in mind, take a moment to be in a comfortable sitting position, relax your body. Take three deep breaths. Picture the person's face in your mind, whatever is the most natural expression for them. If it's smiling, just picture them smiling and continue to take deep long breaths. Notice how you feel, and then send them your gratitude, love and appreciation. Tell them in your mind how you feel about them and what you appreciate about them. If you are in a situation where you can do so, say aloud how you feel about them, and what you are appreciative to them for. They can be close or far away, alive or no longer with us, but trust me, they will receive the message and appreciate it! I do this exercise almost every day.

If you ever feel lonely, try this exercise. It is a life changer! Sometimes I like to add some ritual into this type of exercise by lighting a candle and some incense, turning the lights down and really sending the message to the Universe that I am moving into a sacred space.

Life Experiences Exercise

What are some of your favorite experiences in your life? Would you like more similar experiences, feelings, adventures? Be grateful for the ones you *have* had and then you will be open yourself up to more in the present and future. Choose one experience to focus on for this exercise. Get comfortable, relax your body and take three slow deep breaths. Picture this experience. Who was there? Where were you? At what time of day? What was the weather like? Really take yourself back to that experience. Notice how it makes you feel. Send gratitude to all those who were involved. Really let it sink in. Become open to experiencing more of this type of feeling experience in the present and in the future. Believe that it is possible in your heart and so shall it be.

Compassion for the Self Exercise

What are some of the best things you have done in your life? When have you been the most honorable, loving, compassionate, generous, or supportive? How did that make you feel? Did you really go out of your way to help someone or something else? Whether it was for a friend, family member, stranger or the Earth, pick one of the events, get comfortable, relax your body and take three slow deep breaths and hold the image of this event in your mind's eye. Begin to become grateful to your SELF. Appreciate what you gave to the situation; acknowledge what you did as a good thing, love your Self. Notice how this makes you feel, really stay with this for a few minutes.

It is often hard for us to become grateful to ourselves; however, it is one of the most important aspects of a Gratitude practice. If we cannot become thankful to ourselves, it will be hard for us to ever truly be grateful to anyone else. I find that a fun but more advanced exercise is to do this sitting in front of a mirror, and saying as you look in your own eyes, "I did this for ___, I am grateful to myself for this act, I love my Self, and I am a loving and caring human being."

If you are ever feeling down on yourself, give this exercise a try and watch what happens! I am actually in the middle of donating significant time to someone in need. I don't ask them for any money, I talk to them on the phone a few times a month and I offer them quite a bit of email support. They really need some care, some love, and some guidance. They seem to want this from me and sometimes I will just help someone out of the goodness of my heart. I will do it for weeks or months, just because I can, because I am that abundant, because I know and have faith in that *what I reap, I will sow*. It's a great way for me to appreciate my Self, and really notice the beauty that I give, and have compassion for *me*, Matt O'Grady, the guy who works, who loves, who gives, who receives, who is still aiming higher, opening more, loving deeper.

Earth Appreciation Exercise

I find this exercise to be one of the most fun and super powerful especially if you feel out of sorts, ungrounded, or scattered.

Being grateful to the planet Earth. This is wonderful to do outside on a beautiful day although wherever you are has the same effect. Take some moments to become grounded using the Grounding Exercise above. Notice what is holding you up: a chair, the floor, ground, etc. Sense its temperature, its texture. Feel your whole body and any sensations that you may be experiencing.

Relax the body, take ten deep long slow breaths in and out. Picture the planet in all its glory as if you are in outer space. Notice how majestic and beautiful it is. Send your love and appreciation to it for holding you on it safely all these years. Be grateful to your home, The Grandmother to us all, the planet Earth. Be grateful to her for the air we breathe, the oceans, the trees, planets and animals.

Pick some of your favorite things about our natural world, whether they be waterfalls or forests, mountains or rivers, or double rainbows (YouTube fame). Focus your attention on them and be grateful.

Notice how you feel. Stay in this space as long as you can. This is a great exercise to do if we are feeling overwhelmed, stressed or distracted. Enjoy it!

Chapter 5
Questions and Answers

"Gratitude is the sign of noble souls."
--Aesop

As you work with the principles contained in this book, a bounty of questions will flow forth. Expect that doubt, skepticism, discouragement and disbelief will crop up on occasion as you attempt to adopt new attitudes and habits, and come to accept new results. You may find yourself slipping back to where you were when you first began this book or find that, as your practice deepens, new conundrums arise. Here are my answers to questions most often encountered by clients as they walk the path of living a life of gratitude and appreciation.

Are these principles tied into Buddhism or some other spiritual tradition? Do I have to give up my current religion to practice these principles?

Absolutely not! Gratitude is an energetic opportunity, it is not a religious or philosophical tenet. There are, depending on who is teaching and who is leading, certain religions that focus on gratitude as an important role in how they connect with God and how they demonstrate that they're grateful to God.

In the Catholic religion that I was brought up in, I don't know if I was ever really taught anything about gratitude other than that we were supposed to be grateful, and I'm not even sure if they used the word *grateful*. I remember *thanks*, "give thanks". To give thanks was something I remember hearing in the Catholic religion, which is a nice thing but when there's nothing behind it, no process behind it, no teaching behind it, no learning process to really explain why this matters and what it could lead to, it doesn't give that much inspiration to be thankful.

I think it is far better to cultivate an attitude of gratefulness all the time, which is what they want you to do in the Buddhist temple that I went to for two years in San Diego. They talked about how it helps you relax, helps you just be more connected, and will allow your mediations to have a higher level of energy associated with it, so in the Buddhist tradition, it's already build in there quite a bit.

Currently I do go to a church. It's a Christian church based on the Unity tradition and they focus on gratitude in a tremendous way. It's essentially a new-thought church and so these people believe in the Law of Attraction. They are taught about the Law of Magnetism and they are taught about the power of the mind. Anyone who has studied the power of mind in any detail would have a very difficult time dismissing gratitude and the powers that it can have on our lives.

I can, therefore, act as an example, having known three very different religions which all incorporate a form of gratitude, clearly showing that there's definitely not a specific religious associated with the power of gratitude and appreciation.

If you currently practice a religion, find the overlap between what I'm saying in this book and what your doctrine embraces. You'll find the principles amplified when they're coming not only from your own personal studies, but when you align with a group of people all working together towards the same intention.

I know I'm supposed to be grateful for the smallest of things but when I'm upset or depressed, I can't focus on any of that. What if I can't find anything to feel grateful for?

If you can't find anything to be grateful for, you need to go back to the principle of awareness. If we can't find anything to be grateful for, that means our level of awareness is extremely low and we're extremely caught up in the web of the ego. Awareness can loosen the strength of that web and create some opportunities for us to see beyond this limited outlook.

I always come back to the super basics, which are being grateful for gravity, the breath, having a body, even issues that come along with said body. People who have cancer, people who have been injured in a car accident, people who may even have some sort of significant disability, still have bodies and if you're alive, your body is still working.

I believe whole-heartedly in the practice of gratitude. Being appreciative for what we have despite the appearances is a tremendous opportunity because the gratitude and appreciation that we dive into can significantly affect whatever it is that we see as *wrong* with us. I would debate the view that there is something wrong with us because of pains or disabilities. We are the way that we are, and if there's any hope of changing that, if we have a strong desire to change what we are and it's coming from an authentic place, not a place of lack or need, then appreciation can be the best path towards living that change. Even though it's not always as readily available as we would like it to be, especially when we're in a place of need, so I think that there's always something to be grateful for in every single human being's life.

It's just a matter of awareness and understanding, because if you don't understand that being appreciative could be helpful to your life, then why would you do it? Maybe you think debating, arguing and complaining is going to be helpful to your life. You may even think that if you complain loud enough, someone will hear you and give you what you want. That's often the erroneous belief we form as children, as when we are small, we feel the need to cry, stomp our feet, throw a tantrum, or act sad in order to gain attention, which then elicits a response in our parents and manipulates them into giving us what we want. Yet we still see adults acting in the exact same way and we all know that that is not helpful at all. There's always something to be grateful for.

Meister Eckhart, a German philosopher during the time of the Holy Roman Empire said, "If the only prayer you said in your whole life was, 'Thank You', that would suffice." I've incorporated that, and what a powerful practice.

Here's a great side exercise if this is your issue, and it's the mantra of thank you. I've done this dozens of times where I just sit in meditation. Once I'm in a deep relaxed place, I allow my shoulders to fall, really connecting with my body. Noticing gravity and really allowing my body to connect with the Earth. Feeling the ground, noticing how the breath is flowing in and out of my body and then saying the simple words "thank you."

In the beginning, it may feel silly or there just may not be a strong connection with the words, but continue to repeat them over again. Thank you, thank you, thank you, thank you, thank you. Even letting my body rock a little bit. There's a gentle rhythm along with the words and with the breath. Thank you, thank you, thank you, thank you.

The words almost start to lose the kind of meaning that we're used to when we just say them, but there's some inner process that's happening in the heart center, so after I warm up, so to speak, I'll often put the attention of my mind in my heart center and see what I can feel there. Even as I'm typing these words, I have my left hand placed over my heart, just rubbing in a clockwise motion, and it feels wonderful. This is very gently, very slowly awakening the heart within.

This process can be really helpful to someone who may be practicing appreciation for the first time or who has been in this practice somewhat but needs a quick charge. That *thank you* mediation can really do it for them. I know it's been tremendous for me. Of course, I do that when I'm out on my nature walks as well; looking up to the sky, the trees, nature, just really being appreciative for their presence because they're so beautiful and such a gift to our lives. Not to mention that life on earth would be difficult without those things.

So if you're not finding anything to be grateful for, if you feel fake and like you're just going through the motions of being appreciative, we've all been there, right? Someone gives you something or does something nice for you, but for whatever reason, you're just not that appreciative of it. Well then, you know what it's like to fake it, right? There's a saying in the world of self-development: "Fake it 'til you make it," and there are a lot of benefits to this. I mean, it's not something I would suggest you do all day long, every day of your life, because you're just not living an authentic existence. Often, we need to kick start ourselves and sometimes it's doing the outer stuff to spark the inner stuff. It's to create a new pattern, a new practice.

For example, if it's the first time we've ever shot a basketball, shooting a foul shot can be a lot more difficult than we expect it to be. Or hitting a tennis ball over the net from the back court could be much more difficult than we realize. These are things that we see other people do so easily, but you have to take a practice swing or practice shot, and will still probably miss the first few times. So think of it as practice as opposed to faking it.

I think there's a tremendous amount of focus put on tangible truth, and what we're working with here is spiritual truth. We're working outside of time to connect with our source. Essentially, that's really what appreciation practice entails — the alignment of that energy you are connecting to with that source. Any time you are grateful for something, you allow that beauty to arise within you, you are connecting with God, with a Source, with the Force, the absolute Allah, Yahweh, or Buddha. Whatever you want to call it, you're connecting with it in those moments.

You mentioned feeling grateful, even if you're suffering from a disease or tragedy. How can we be expected to feel grateful for bad things happening to us or our loved ones?

Well, this one can be really tough, especially right at the beginning. An example that I use is when my grandmother died. She was ninety-six. It was 'expected', based on her age and how her health had deteriorated over time, and therefore I had a lot of prep time to emotionally deal with her passing. I was grateful for her and our connection even before she passed.

I was also there when she passed. My mom was there as well and there's this real beauty of being there. I was very quickly able to get into a grateful space for all the time we spent together. I had known her all my life and was very appreciative to her for different things that I had experienced with her. As much as I missed her and felt a deep loss because I missed her spicy personality, there was also an immediacy of appreciation for the time that we were able to spend together, especially during the last few years of her life.

That's an example that I use, because even in death, we can be grateful. If we know how to direct our focus and attention towards the goodness that we *did* have with someone we can find things to be grateful for.

I'm not saying that this is the easiest practice or that someone can even start their practice while dealing with death or other tragedy. The point I'm trying to make is that, yes this is tough, but because of some upfront work, I was able to respond to my grandmother's death the way I was. Instead of focusing on, "Oh, she's gonna die, how will I cope without her here?" I focused on the occasions I saw her during the time that I did have with her. I stopped thinking about her physical presence no longer being in my life and focused more on her spirit and the beauty of the connection I had with her.

I've been able to do this with a few deaths now, although not as quickly. Sometimes it takes a little while for me to work towards the gratitude. I don't think there is anything wrong with that. We are still human beings and I've never said that this appreciation practice will be immediate in all situations. It's just not realistic to expect it. Contrast is a big part of life and it's actually an important part that helps us grow. So there's nothing wrong with that process of needing to get into the space of or coming around to being appreciative. Be patient with yourself as you go through this practice.

What happens if I feel grateful for the wrong things? For instance, feeling grateful that something bad happened to someone else?

It's funny, I was just thinking about this recently. I call this the 'lowest grade gratitude possible' because in a way, there needed to be some sort of wish for something bad to happen to someone, even if initially it's an unconscious one. I know I've felt in the past that, "Oh, they got what they deserved" kind of feeling or self-righteousness. I don't think that's really gratitude. Strictly speaking, I guess you could call it the lowest grade gratitude, which isn't really the type of gratitude and appreciation that I'm discussing in this book.

What I refer to is of a fine beautiful pure energy. If you're seeing something bad happening to someone, whether physically, emotionally or otherwise, and you feel glad that it happened, that really doesn't feel like gratitude to me. Essentially, if you're wishing bad things on a person, which I think we all know if you've embraced any of this book thus far, that's really not the direction we're going in. It's much better to be happy about or grateful for what happens in their life, regardless of what it is. However, that's not really the gratitude or appreciation I'm talking about here either. Not that you can't do it, but what I'm really talking about is a self-knowing process. Knowing thyself through a gratitude process with focus on our own life, because that's where gratitude really starts and ends, is in our own life, in our own hearts.

At the same time, I've felt that a pattern builds up around certain people, sometimes certain famous people that you hear about, supposed dictators or terrible people who then get taken down or killed, and there is this immediate kind of pattern of, "I'm glad they got them," or, "It serves them right".

However, I've really tried to diffuse that spontaneous and negative response over the last couple of decades since my time in the military. It really is a great pattern to release. I find that when things like that do come up and I don't have that reaction anymore, I'm so grateful that it's absent in me. I can just turn my attention back towards what I *want* to see in my life rather than what I don't want to see. The taking down of bad people gives me no joy. It did when I was younger, I admit, but it was not a high energy, and I am interested in focusing on high and divine energies.

Okay, I've incorporated the exercises of living gratitude and appreciation into my life on a daily process. What's next on my path of growth?

More gratitude and appreciation! This is not a process that ever gets stagnant or old. It's a practice that we can take with us to our last moment on this planet and hopefully beyond. It would certainly make sense to me that living in gratitude is a big part of what we experience when we're out of the physical body. However, if you're seeking a more concrete answer, when in mediation, or some quiet space, ask your inner self or higher self what's next for you. Ask your guardians or your guides or whoever it is you pray to, connect with your ancestors, or God, or Jesus or Buddha, whoever, and ask them for guidance.

I believe that there's a tremendous amount of different directions we can go into spiritually. One of the things that I love to work on with people once they feel like they've fully understood and practiced gratitude and appreciation to the hilt (which I don't really think is ever truly possible), is the practice of forgiveness. That will be covered in my next book!

Because I think that almost everyone has someone whom they find difficult to forgive and that's where our work comes in, as if we're able to release that resentment, we've released some of the largest baggage that is possible to have in life. Holding that grudge or possibly hatred towards someone causes our lives to ripple in ways we can't imagine, until we are capable of forgiving and have forgiven again and again. Forgiveness is a tremendously beautiful practice. I highly recommend it.

I've found I want to record the things I'm grateful for. How do you keep a gratitude journal?

A gratitude journal is a really wonderful practice. I think there's a few different ways to pursue this. I have one gratitude journal into which I just write really quick insights. It's a small, beautiful book that was given to me by a good friend I've worked with for many years. She gave it to me when she was on a trip to Costa Rica and it's made from banana paper, so it's kind of cool. I quickly write down spontaneous thoughts such as "I'm grateful for the sun. I'm grateful for the smell of grass. I really appreciate that I have running water." You can jot down things that people have said or people have done, or just aspects of life that you really enjoy and want to document.

Then I have another journal, a bigger one which has more room to write in. I'll often write what I'm grateful for in a poetic prose kind of way and allow that to really work within me. If we can do even a minute or two of gratitude journaling per day, I think that's a tremendous practice. I've done it many times during my life and have found it to be tremendously helpful.

Chapter 6

Gratitude Practice for Practitioners and Groups

"I don't have to chase extraordinary moments to find happiness - it's right in front of me if I'm paying attention and practicing gratitude."

--Brene Brown

If you are a spiritual healer, body worker, consultant or coach, consider introducing techniques for increasing gratitude into your offerings, if you're not already. In working with clients both individually and in groups, I've found that doing work around gratitude and appreciation serves my clients in multiple ways. For example, this can quickly raise client's vibrations.

As healers, we are aware of the results of being around people vibrating at lower frequencies. Before I begin with my clients, I like to do some gratitude and appreciation exercises so that their energy is raised and then we can proceed. It provides a demonstrable change in their emotions and thoughts. .When a client is in the depth of despair and can't see anything positive in their life, walking through a basic appreciation exercise can help them change their focus from what's going wrong to what they have to be thankful for. This is a powerful way to demonstrate the control they have over their emotional state.

Prepare them for future work: By reframing the current experience of their life, doing work in gratitude can open your clients' eyes to what they stand to gain by changing their attitude in other areas. By making this initial shift, they'll be more open to future exercises and practices you will introduce.

Enable them to make bigger breakthroughs: It may sound crazy, but we should be grateful for just having the opportunity to be grateful! As your clients experience insights and transformations around their issues, the practice of gratitude amplifies their revelations. So not only do they become appreciative of the breakthroughs in and of themselves, they also feel gratitude for the opportunity your work together affords to receive the breakthroughs in the first place.

The following tips I provide are not intended to be a training manual or formal prescription for conducting healing work. These are simple tips that I've gleaned in the course of working with numerous clients, facilitating spiritual and emotional change, which *do* work.

Encourage them to participate in fun activities to lighten their mood: Sometimes things are tough and can be sad and depressing but we have to counteract that and one great way is by partaking in what I call the Laughter Exercise, which we have covered previously. Find comedians that we like, actors and movies that we think are funny, people that make us laugh. We all have that person who just cracks us up and so we should invite our clients to tap into this source.

Assign your client the simple task of making a list of the movies, books, people, websites, plays that make them laugh. Another idea is to put together a clip or an assortment of funny scenes from movies. Everyone's humor and taste is different, so this might have the desired effect. Look for classic slapstick humor like the Honeymooners, Laurel and Hardy, or the Three Stooges to err on the safe side.

Coach your clients to smile at things they don't like. Studies have shown that even though it feels very fake, plastic and not very real at first, you will begin to laugh at yourself for even smiling during the situation and all of a sudden, this huge burden is lifted. A smile or laugh is basically channeling joy and appreciation for something that's funny when we laugh, when we smile. Especially in a group setting, the contagion of laughter will serve to elevate participants' mood and vibration.

Help them to appreciate one another: This is a great exercise to use as an opener for a group, or even during individual sessions. The discussion of what we're all grateful for in our lives and what we're grateful for in a group really brings people down to the human being next to them, or the human being that they're connected to. Being grateful right in front of the people that we work with or are connected to is really tremendous. You have no idea how many people rarely hear sincere words of appreciation.

Have your group begin by taking a few minutes to write down something they appreciate about someone in the group. You can also pair people up and have them list three things they appreciate about the other person. I guarantee that if there is any dissention or friction among the group, it will melt in the face of sincere gratitude. This is an effective technique for conflict resolution because it breaks the ice and quickly takes people to a place of warmth that sets the tone for more productive healing work. If you're working one on one with a client who is suffering from low self-esteem for example or who sees themselves in a negative light, take them through the process of concocting a list of things they appreciate about themselves.

Encourage specificity—whether it's appreciating their feet for carrying them up and down stairs, their eyes for allowing them to see the color of rainbows and grass, their lungs for allowing them to breathe...The list goes on. Encourage them to come up with as many things about their existence as they can to appreciate. Assign them the task to read this list every day until your next session and to report back on the quality of their day and their experiences with it.

In a group setting, you can write the appreciation points on a whiteboard or flip pad and assign each person to write down what others appreciated about them to read daily. To take this a step further, in a group setting after your work is done, you can facilitate the group using this as an opportunity to build even further.

For example, when you know what someone else appreciates, you're really getting to know an important part of who they are and you might even be able to provide the opportunity for them to be more appreciative. If you know someone's favorite coffee, to pick a simple example, you could bring it to them. You could surprise them with it. You could do that once a month or once a week or whenever is appropriate, so they know that you appreciate them. Imagine the group dynamic in a workplace or other group setting that embraced these practices!

Earth Appreciation Exercise: This is a powerful exercise to do one-on-one with clients or as a group on a beautiful day. Meet your client(s) in a natural setting or step outside to a peaceful area near your work location. Take some moments to ground yourself, using the previously mentioned Grounding Exercise.

Walk your client through everything you observe. Call their attention to their feelings and any sensations they're experiencing. Guide them through breathing exercises to usher in a feeling of relaxation and tranquility. Ask them to close their eyes and picture the planet in all its glory, as if you are in outer space. Ask them to notice how majestic and beautiful the earth is, send their love and appreciation to it for holding them safely all these years.

Explain that we're grateful to our home, the Mother of us all, the planet Earth. We're grateful to her for the air we breathe, the oceans, the plants and animals. Ask the participants to open their eyes and pick some of their favorite aspects of the natural world, whether waterfalls or forests, mountains or rivers or double rainbows, and focus your attention on them and be grateful, especially for anything which appears within view of your location. Ask your clients to take note of how they feel and to stay in this space for as long as they can. Advise them that this is a great exercise to do no matter where they are, when they're feeling overwhelmed, stressed or distracted.

Additional group exercises—Matt's tips for facilitating healing when working with clients: It's crucial that you bring gratitude and appreciation into your own work because the clients who allow you to serve them afford you so many opportunities. More usefully, heightening your appreciation of your clients can elevate your skills.

I used to be a massage therapist, and one of the things that I did right before I worked on someone, even before I placed my hands on them, was to sense their energy with my hands just a few inches away from their body. I would say a prayer to guide me to the highest good for this person and for myself, through the act of massage. I would be grateful. I would honor them lying there, coming to work with me in this way, allowing themselves to be vulnerable lying there in their partially-clothed state with their eyes closed. The whole process involves tremendous trust and so I would honor the trust they had to put themselves in this position with me and asked to be able to provide them with the absolute best that I had available, as far as massage goes.

There was some energy work involved there. It was really the getting to that state of appreciation right before I put my hands on someone and I've had many clients say to me, "You know, there's just something about your hands," but it wasn't my hands. It was the energetic state I was able to summon and channel through my hands that my clients felt. That's why I had a thriving massage practice with consistent clients who really appreciated the service, purely because of that.

This is one of the methods which holistic practitioners can use, just by asking their clients what they're grateful for and expressing to them at the same time that they're grateful for their patronage, thus creating a circle of appreciation that is a sure fire road to prosperity and a successful business.

What to do if you're dealing with resistance: Resistance will inevitably come up. It's just a natural process of us working on ourselves, developing ourselves, connecting with source. Resistance is a form of contrast that arises, sometimes called the 'second force' in Gurdjieffian philosophy.

This force of resistance is useful in allowing us the opportunity to think about our true intentions, as we take a step forward, whether that's a physical step or an internal, emotional, energetic step. Resistance often occurs at that moment when we embark on something like an appreciation process. When it happens, our instinct is to throw up our hands in defeat and walk away, but our resolve is like a muscle being built so that any of this defiance experienced gives us the opportunity to work against it, thus making us stronger.

Think about resistance as like a weight; for example,

when you're doing a bench press. If we work with resistance that we can handle, those appreciation muscles, if you will, get stronger and stronger and then we are able to deal with greater resistance.

I really don't think we get resistance that we can't handle. It's really much more about the story that we tell ourselves and the beliefs that we have about certain situations, subjects and people. Essentially, a pattern has built up over time that's really only there because it involves thoughts that we've been thinking constantly throughout our lives.

An example that I like to think of is a plow moving across a field. As it moves in the same pattern through the field, it delves deeper and deeper, until that pattern becomes so deep that you couldn't get out of it unless you stood on your ox and climbed out. We therefore have to find ways of revising these patterns and developing new ones. We can do this by using a trial and error method or by trying something totally new in order to create a different pathway, even if it doesn't always necessarily feel exactly right or we're not quite sure what we're being drawn into.

One of the most powerful things that I've experienced in my life—and I'm sure part of it's based on my personality, how I was brought up and the fact that my dad always encouraged me to try different food—is trying something new.

The willingness to try something new is a great practice for anyone that's interested in really connecting with themselves. Now, I'm not saying, if you have a fear of heights that brings on convulsions, sweats and the urge to vomit, that you should just handle it. I'm not suggesting that at all. I'm suggesting that you work with what you have.

It's the simple things, like trying a different way home from work. We all usually know the way home and take a certain route most of the time. Most people will go the same way all of the time, but I don't. I try different ways, even if they take a few minutes longer. If it's going to take several hours longer, then I'm probably not going to try it, or at least not often, but never be afraid to try different ways of doing things. If you always drive but you could take the train every now and again, take the train. It gives you a new perspective on life and breaks the monotony of routine.

Just try something new. If for example you say hello the same way all the time—"hey, how ya doing?"—try something different and perhaps say, "Good morning, how are you today?"

If you wear the same kind of clothes all the time, same color or same style, try something just a little bit more unusual for you. I really like blues and greens, grays, and blacks. Those are like my colors. That's really what I like. It's what I like to wear. I mean, I'll wear white, but I'm not really into orange and yellow and red, but every once in a while I will just step out of my comfort zone and buy a yellow shirt. Once I've got it on, I usually really like it.. It does us good to do something slightly adventurous and it's such a confidence builder. We start to realize that the experience isn't too terrible after all.

I recommend that you start to make really simple changes in your life. Food is a tremendous opportunity to experiment in this way. If you tend to only like roast beef, then make an effort to try something else. There are a lot of cold cuts available. If you only like certain fruits, go ahead and try a couple of other ones. If you only like certain nuts, go ahead and try other nuts. If you only like a certain kind of pasta sauce, try a different sauce every once in a while.

I understand it's comforting to know what you're dealing with and to enjoy that one particular thing but it won't kill you I promise.

Of course, that does depend on what the practice is. I'm not referring to anything involving violence or guns or anything like that, just something that's really simple like eating or driving home, and then you can build up to doing many different things. It's interesting and reminds me of the question about what's next after gratitude. Keep practicing gratitude and appreciation of your life in different ways and the different things you have in your life, which will then lead you to what's next.

Gratitude Stories from Friends and Colleagues

Toni V. Martin

I see gratitude as the notion that we were created by a higher power and gratitude is a way to thank and show appreciation to God for the blessings we've been given. Acknowledging the good things we've been given through our actions, words, and thoughts. Reflecting on our blessings and taking the time to say thank you. I have a tendency to see the glass as half empty and have therefore come to use gratitude as a way to shift my perspective on things I see as dissatisfying.

I am constantly trying to use gratitude as a way to humble myself and to be happy with the basics. I used to flip out when bad things happened or when things didn't go the way I wanted. However, since I've learned to look for the blessings and lessons in every situation, I am a lot more mellow! I have learned that things could always be worse. When I don't get what I want, I've learned to be thankful for what I *do* have and reflecting on that makes me happier and richer. It really is amazing!

Through my spiritual path of Christianity, I've developed a close connection with God. I've encountered people, such as my pastor and therapist, who have helped me to learn how to choose my thoughts with care and who have explained the benefits of living a humbled life. More recently, I've learned from Matt O'Grady, who has shown me such practical and simple ways to incorporate practices of gratitude and appreciation. I feel empowered and in touch with God when I use these principles. I have used them to help others see things in a new light, and I know there are more realms I can explore with these principles.

Lisa Dorey

The word *gratitude* presents a very solid, tangible image to me. Words springing to mind include *cornerstone, foundation* and *DNA spiral in the core of my being.* I'd define it as being aware and thankful for the key people in my life, for the home I live in and the air that I breathe. Gratitude is embedded at such a deep level in my heart that I couldn't imagine even existing without it.

If gratitude is my foundation, then appreciation has a lighter touch. It is the feel of a warm woolly scarf against my skin, it is the soft, warm summer breeze in my hair and the taste of a delicious juicy peach, almost impossible to eat without juice flowing everywhere on the first bite!

The first step to really live a life of gratitude and appreciation is to slow down enough to notice them. We live our lives at such a frantic pace that we often don't make time to even notice all the wonderful things in our life, let alone be grateful for them. Once you practice the art of stillness, of being, of living in the moment, we can really start to be aware of all the wonderful people, events and joy that surround us.

Getting out into nature every day, watching the seasons do their work, seeing leaves fall, noticing the harsh winter frost, watching the stirrings of new life in spring and the blossoming into full abundance is a truly magical thing. Nature doesn't rush; it has its own time, its perfection and its rhythm.

Being able to observe the Universe in this manner embodies gratitude by being thankful for my very existence within this wonderful framework. I have learned to live more in the moment, savoring what is happening now, as opposed to rushing on to the next thing on my 'to- do- list'.

I have really learnt to appreciate the journey of life and take so much more from life itself by seeing the gifts presented to me. In the past, I'd have been rushing too fast to even notice there was a gift there at all! I believe we act like human magnets, attracting more of what we are and as I have moved to a more thankful attitude, the Universe has provided me more to be thankful for. So many wonderful things have come into my life; more harmonious relationships with the special people in my life, a job where I am nourished at a soul level by what I do, working with a fantastic network of like-minded individuals, who continually lift and support one another, and constantly being surprised by unexpected events which I could not have conceived.

I have always read widely on the subject of personal development. This, in time, built into becoming a Reiki Master, a Pranic Healer and an Energy Healer working with Archangels. By practicing a life living in peace and joy, gratitude has become a natural way of being ... and I am eternally grateful for my personal transformation!

Jennifer Urezzio
http://www.knowsoulslanguage.net

A deep feeling of being in connection with the Divine and appreciation for that connection

Gratitude, for me, has to be an everyday practical experience. I take time each morning and evening to list what I'm grateful for and when someone does something that I'm grateful for, I let them know! I enjoy life more. I'm in present time and challenges are met with a feeling of discovery and love for myself and for others. I also know deep down that I'm one with the Divine and my life is an experience of this belief.

Gratitude for me was about self-discovery. I used to do gratitude really, really fast just so I could get to the complaints. "Hey, God, thanks so much for the six new clients today, but why didn't the possible Client Number Seven want to work with me? I'm still not feeling or getting enough!" That was how I was expressing gratitude. I wasn't fully present or focused on the amazing moments of my life. I was putting all my power behind the struggle. So I began a journey to practice gratitude in a way that resonated with me. Not the way I was told, not the way the books said or my spiritual mentor suggested, but the way that resonated with me mind, body and spirit.

Jenn Edden

http://www.jecoaching.com

Gratitude is, for me, 'intense feelings of love'. It's a heart-warming experience that wells up in my body and gives me a sense of well-being and peace, deep within when I bring to mind something or someone that has impacted my life in a positive way. I have immense gratitude for my husband, who gives me the space to grow in ways that I need to in order to live my life's purpose. Just thinking of him brings me a deep sense of peace and gratefulness.

Appreciation goes hand in hand with gratitude for me. As a heart-centered entrepreneur and coach—whose maiden name just happens to translate into passion—I define appreciation as more of an intense feeling in my body than actual words on a page. When I'm being appreciated, it's a sense that I am loved or that I send love to the person I am appreciating. It's a way of being.

Appreciating someone through words and actions to show love. I live them. Period. I know through the Law of Attraction "that which you put out, you get back". Therefore, I find reasons THROUGHOUT EACH DAY to thank (and bless) people everywhere. Our planet is hurting and I decided years ago that I can contribute to a NEW MOVEMENT OF PEACE & LOVE by being that in the world.

I am extra nice, complementary to people who I can see are directing their anger at me in stores, while driving, telemarketers, etc. They are the ones who need the most love directed towards them.

When I'm having an off day for no reason apparent to me, I tend to APPRECIATE myself more that day knowing my head trash is at an all-time high. This helps me stay in the flow regardless of what my mind is doing that day.

My relationship with my husband is off-the-charts amazing from our sex, to our overall loveyness after being married for ten years, we are kind to each other regardless of how 'off' our day might have been. We give ourselves the freedom to do what we need to do to take care of ourselves. Our marriage is like a beautiful dance!!

My biz is ROCKIN'. I create programs and people come. They see results, they refer me...it just flows...and along with that is the money aspect. That flows too...after all MONEY is just energy. My body is in the best shape of my life after having two kids...being appreciative of myself melts fat off your body. Seriously. I look forward to every day as a new adventure...worries are gone. Period. I know in my heart that I am deserving of whatever it is I choose to ask for. For this I am grateful.

As a highly sensitive person, when I allow myself to get quiet and I am off the sugar, no joke it's true, just ask any one of my 21-day Reclaim Your MOJO Challengers....it just COMES TO ME. My inner guide talks and I am reminded of my TRUTH. Also, reading tons of books on spirituality and receiving DAILY LOA emails from Abraham for the past 3 years has been a life changer. I don't miss a day. Ever.

Philip Giuliano

For me, it's being thankful for everything my life—for that which feels good and even that which doesn't, since I know that will bring growth and new desire for expansion. Seeing the perfection in all situations. Acknowledging that life is perfectly imperfect—challenges are designed into the program and we need them. I try and take some time in every day to focus on Gratitude and Appreciation, to project that energy in my world and use it to soothe myself when challenges arise. I find it helpful to make a mental, if not actual, list of everything I feel appreciation for in that moment.

I find that life becomes easier—the challenges are met more gracefully. I see that new opportunities seem to blossom all the time with just a few minutes of focused appreciation. Through my spiritual practices mostly—much came from channeled teachers like AA Michael, St Germain, Emmanuel, Seth and Abraham. Of course.

Gratitude and Appreciation, like love and joy, is its own reward. We all have so much in our lives to feel Gratitude and Appreciation0 for, and that act brings relief and a better vibration in on itself. It need not be a means to an end—though it can be, since it is the fast track for creating more things to feel good about in our lives. In the end, nothing is more important than feeling good, and nothing does that better than cultivating an "attitude of gratitude".

Sophie Mihalko
http://www.SophieMihalko.com

The energy of recognizing that something exists and its mere existence expands my life. It is the most delicious form of overcoming resistance, allowing everything to be. Choosing to see the positive qualities and traits of something or someone, I wake up every morning asking myself "who do I choose to be today?" When I realize how much I can be, I have a big smile on my face, so grateful for me. I also use gratitude any time I can sense my thoughts going toward, "I wish it was different." When my daughter continues to play instead of getting dressed for school, I am grateful that she has made something that feels good a priority in her life. But I have also noticed that being aware of something without judging it in any way (whether good or bad) is the greatest form of gratitude. I most often seek gratitude energy while I'm waiting in traffic. There is nothing to do but sit there. I let myself be in the moment, without judging anything and within seconds, I will find a new road that flows, or traffic will lighten up. But I am still grateful, still happy to practice gratitude as I wait. I am so much more relaxed! I am not stressing out about anything being "not the way it should be." Gratitude and appreciation don't quite allow that I am also much more aware. Before, I would have concluded something as good or bad. Now I ask, "How can I be grateful about this?" and I become aware of what the Universe has been diligently delivering to me. It started with the Law of Attraction, to attract more to be grateful for, but I am now an Access Consciousness Bars Facilitator, and through my classes, I discovered that the energy of gratitude is so potent that it is in perfect vibration with my body. How does it get any better than that? Every 10 seconds we can make a different choice. Choosing gratitude does not mean that I cannot choose awareness 10 seconds later. I may choose the energy of gratitude repeatedly, but I always have a choice and I am very grateful for that.

Karen Garvey

http://www.TheAnswersUnlimited.com

Gratitude to me is experiencing a sense that everything is good in the world. It's a feeling of contentment, a knowingness that my path has brought to me the people, circumstances, and ideas that parallel me with my soul's intent. Appreciation is the act of focusing on something and taking account of its goodness. It's about seeing the value and positive qualities in a happening, a person, or a path. Day-to-day life makes it easy to overlook the best attributes of what's going on around us, but to appreciate means to pause, look, pay attention, and value what is there.

Practicing gratitude in a meaningful way for me means not only remembering what good is in my life, but also about feeling the goodness. I get a certain buzz when I feel good. It's like that feeling when a star-crossed couple finally gets together at the end of a movie, or the chills from a really great Hallmark commercial. I pursue whatever brings that feeling. I earnestly submerse myself in being grateful for these moments.

By being conscious that they exist, I notice the moments more. Being thankful from my mind does not emit the same powerful energy that being thankful from my whole being emits. I let waves of contentment wash over me like a twilight blanket covers the earth each night. For me, being appreciative and grateful has been a natural process after discovering principles of universal wisdom. The more I understand the meaning behind our journey on earth and understand our interconnectedness, the more easily I feel appreciative of my life's circumstances. Appreciation and gratitude play a role in a much greater shift, all of which bring me to increasing peace and happiness.

The change began when I 'received' simultaneous information about the attack on the World Trade Center during 9-11, and opened to a surprising intuitive ability that I vigorously pursued because of the value of the messages—the information I got was optimistic, hopeful, and gave explanations for the underlying eternal value for events that we cannot necessarily make sense of on earth. One of the defining principles I discovered is that we are all doing the best we can within in our level of awareness. Remembering this fact makes it easier to feel grateful for all circumstances around me.

Now as an Intuitive, Speaker, Author, Personal & Professional Coach, I use my conduit to universal knowledge to provide ongoing insights for workshops, media appearances, and books. I bring forth principles of enlightenment (such as the value of appreciation and gratitude) and methods to achieve them.

Stephanie Pedersen
http://www.HighImpactHealth.com

Gratitude is such an interesting word for me. I grew up in a very observant Mormon home. For us, gratitude had a slight twinge of obligation that went along with it. One of the worst things we could be called was *ingrate*—literally, one without gratitude for those things given to him or her. So to be grateful, meant to be in service to whomever or whatever gave us the gifts we were grateful for.

Fast forward to today, and I no longer associate myself with a specific religion, nor do I see gratitude as a subservient, groveling form of thankfulness. I see it as clear sight. Yes, clear sight. I can clearly see this and this and that, that event over there and that person back there. I can clearly see the good, the opportunities, the disappointments that turned out to be gifts and the perceived wrong turns that actually lead to open doors I wasn't sure I wanted to go through at the time, but after doing so, experienced an enormous shift in some part of my life. Gratitude is clear sight. Noticing the good and acknowledging that these things have shown up in my life.

In my vocabulary, appreciation is an action word. I am grateful for this person, and I show my appreciation by thanking the divine for bringing him or her into my life. I show my appreciation by directly telling this wonderful person how thankful I am to have them close. I appreciate my children's wonderful school, so I go there and volunteer. I want to give the staff the same loving energy they give my children. I give a donation to a particular cause because I appreciate the work they do and want to show them my feelings.

I am a big believer in action. I am a 'pray for potatoes with a hoe in your hand' kind of woman! I incorporate gratitude and appreciation into my life every single day with action. I actively look for things to be grateful for. Sure, there are always the big ones—the ones you don't even need to search for something to feel grateful for. Things like your partner, your children, your family, your good friends, a job you love, having a roof over your head and enough to eat are wonderful things to be grateful for, but it is important for me to go deeper. Each evening I make 'a grateful list'. What happened or who appeared in my day that I am grateful for. *Maybe i*t might be something like, "It rained. If it hadn't rained, I would never have jumped on that bus and run into my roommate from 15 years ago whom I had lost touch with." Or, "I am grateful that my boss is out on vacation, so I had the chance to take a full hour's long lunch with two coworkers whom I've never had the chance to get to know."

Appreciation for me is making a motion to show someone (even if that someone is "just" the Universe), that I am thankful of those things that came into my life. It could be a prayer, thanking the Universe for giving me the chance to meet with those two coworkers. It could be actually saying to a person, "I really appreciate the way you are always so cheerful and upbeat." It could be sending a card, writing out a check, signing a petition, offering an extra hug, sitting still and listening—anything that says, "Thank you. I care."

Since becoming more consciously grateful and appreciative, the Universe has given me more. It's as if someone out there loves being thanked, loves being praised, so is giving me even more, just to experience gratitude and appreciation, and really, isn't that the way all living things work? You praise a puppy for bringing you a newspaper and soon the pup is looking for every opportunity possible to bring you something so it can get another dose of praise. You thank a child for a job well done and suddenly, the child is happily doing more of whatever it is will get you to thank him again.

I went through a deeply unhappy period in my late 20s, where I wanted what everyone else had. I compared myself to this person and to that person. I couldn't figure out why he or she had something I so desperately wanted. I studied everything I could get my hands on that may lead me to an answer.

What finally helped was a thin volume by Florence Scoville Shinn called *The Game of Life*. I realized that, although I never complained aloud, I was still complaining in my head and that counted. I realized I was focused on all I wanted but didn't have. I realized that you attract to you the things you put your attention and your action on. I slowly began to notice and fall in love with what was working in my life, I began to appreciate those who were already in my orbit and I began to see the opportunities right in front of me. The Universe loves a generous person and decided to give me more.

I am truly the luckiest woman in the world. People talk a lot about the Law of Attraction; how it works, how it doesn't work, how it is hard, how you have to do it like this, or like that, but here's the thing: the Law of Attraction is built on two very easy, non-complicated actions: Gratitude and Appreciation. Noticing and thanking. Seeing and doing. Not hard, is it? It makes you and everyone around you, feel so good.

Here's a challenge for you: for one full week, notice everything. Say thank you for everything. At the end of the week, look back. Do you feel different? Happier? More full? Is your life bigger and brighter? It may be worth continuing for the rest of your life!

Lynn Keating

Gratitude is about always keeping the sacredness of life close. It is thankfulness for what *is*, without any expectation of what it *should* be. It is seeing the gift in both the miracles and the imperfections.

Appreciation is the act of honoring the goodness, grace and beauty around you by trying to be present and embrace the realness of what is, here and now, to feel thankful of whatever life brings, as it means I have another day to be here. Trying to take every opportunity to send a thank you or tell someone what they mean to me. To know that all of what is experienced has the potential to shape and deepen understanding and compassion for myself and others. I believe by truly hearing and seeing another person and understanding their story, it allows me to see life from many perspectives and opens me up to a greater awareness of another's experience. This in turn, is a reminder of how big life is...which only opens up more doors and windows to seeing grace and glimpsing all that there is to be thankful for in this life.

I love and cherish every moment to the best of my ability. Gratitude helps me keep perspective on what is truly important and what is good right now. I believe my anxiety, which I struggled with for many years after my dad died, lessened significantly. Instead of worrying about every symptom being some undiagnosed illness or who I might unexpectedly lose next, I began to focus on everyone who was in my life and to appreciate the time I was given with them.

By allowing myself to be present and grateful, I found myself worrying less about "What if?" There is no question that

I initially learned the concept from my parents. I also recall being told a story about my grandmother, who suffered a long terminal illness in her early 40's: In the hospital, when asked by someone, "Why is this happening to you?" her response was, "Why not me?"

As a child, I was struck by that...why would any of us be immune to pain? Those words awoke me to the fact that we do not know what each day may bring. However, we do have a choice in how we view the world and how we live our life. My awareness deepened after my dad took his life when I was 10. In my grief and pain, I shut down and turned inward; I will never forget and always be grateful for the kindness and compassion of those who loved me enough to stand with and love me through it.

I realized it was possible to be sad for all that I lost but also be grateful for all I was given. The beauty about gratitude is that it is so big that it can exist alongside any other feeling. I feel being grateful allows for feelings of joy, sadness, anger, hurt, disappointment, fear...while also recognizing that goodness and grace can co-exist—whether it be in sunlight, a smile, a laugh, a friend, a child, a pet, any tiny glimmer of hope, something for which to be thankful.

Like William Blake said in his famous poem, "To See a World..."

> To see a world in a grain of sand, And a
> Heaven in a wild flower,
> Hold infinity in the palm of your hand,
> And eternity in an hour.

Loni Markman

Gratitude means thankfulness, appreciating what you have, noticing simple pleasures and acknowledging everything that you receive. It means learning to live your life as if everything were a miracle and being aware on a continuous basis of how much you've been given. Gratitude shifts your focus from what your life lacks to the abundance that is already present.

Being appreciative allows you to focus on the positive and not dwell on the negative. It means having an emotion that has the power to attract what you desire and bring even more happiness into your life. When we appreciate who we are, what we have, a beautiful scenery or moment with our friends, family and even strangers, there becomes a lightness in our lives, our days becomes brighter and the universe opens up showing us so much more beauty in the world than before.

I first started practicing gratitude around my body as I was trying to learn to love and appreciate myself instead of punish myself. Once I experienced the power this had over my relationship to my body, I started to use it in all areas of life. I focus on gratitude as a daily practice and I use it all the time in my practice helping women learn to create a better relationship to food and their bodies through nutrition and mindset. I am not a big mediator and I thought that creating an attitude of gratitude would be difficult because of that, but it was simply not true.

A few things I do to incorporate these principles include programming my phone to have little gratitude reminders like, "Who does not thank for little will not thank for much," or, "I am grateful for being me," and I have them set to randomly pop up as daily reminders. When I first started, I used to keep a gratitude journal and now this is something I have all my clients do. I make sure to consciously choose my words and try to say only things that are positive and loving.

I also take the time to share my appreciation and give thanks for those in my life. Nothing makes me happier than to let someone I care about know just how great they are or to make a stranger smile. I've experienced a new sense of self and appreciation for my own body while being able to share my gift of helping women learn to love themselves and nourish themselves. I have healed many relationships using the Law of Attraction and replacing anger with appreciation.

As far as I can remember, I would always say I was a positive person but I read a book in 2000 called *Excuse Me, Your Life is Waiting* by Lynn Gabhorn, and that really propelled me to dive in deeper.

Just as a nutrition and weight loss coach, I have seen first-hand how powerful our mindset can be and how it can actually change our physical body. I think if we were grateful for the blessing we do have in our lives, we would be more fulfilled and less "hungry." This is key to lasting weight loss. We must learn to love and appreciate what is, in order to move into any permanent change.

Jeannette Maw
http://www.goodvibecoach.com

Gratitude is something I feel when I consciously recognize something that makes my life better. I know some do, but I don't personally make a big distinction between gratitude and appreciation. Appreciation is a feeling I have for something that makes my life more enjoyable, rewarding, satisfying, etc.

I aspire to be more conscious about what I'm grateful for, in order to more regularly feel appreciation. Life is so much easier to enjoy! It's easier to see things that feel good, it's easier to see how things are going 'right', it's easier to be happy being here.

The most profound experiences of feeling appreciation that I've had were when I found my way there very deliberately and consciously in situations that, at the outset, didn't seem to warrant appreciation, like when my crackhead neighbor was making death threats, or when my boyfriend was breaking up with me, etc. In those times, to purposely choose appreciation in the turmoil and the contrast led to some of the best experiences and relationships of my life. Appreciation is pure magic.

Chapter 7
Bringing it All Together

"If the only prayer you say in your life is 'thank you', that would suffice."

--Meister Eckhart

I hope you have enjoyed this book, and I have a divine wish that it helps you in your daily life for many years to come. However, I know there are millions of books telling us billions of things that we can do to help our lives, and it's not always so easy deciding what is best for us, how to do it etc. With that in mind, this chapter is about Bringing it All Together in a Daily Practice. Consider this quote by Anton Chekhov:

Knowledge is of no value unless you put it into practice.

Your practice does not have to be just when you block out time to do yoga, relax, meditate, pray, visualize, etc. It can be integrated throughout your day so it simply becomes a part of your daily life. This way, you do not need to put in a whole lot of extra effort, you are just inviting in a healthier, happier way of going about your life. Below I list different times, situations and opportunities to bring your practice together into one integrated whole, sometimes known as...Your Life.

Morning

I am a big believer in thinking about what we want most for our lives at least twice per day, and those two times bookend our days. When we first awake is a superbly fertile time to practice, because we are fresh from our rest, our mental slate is clean, we have not taken on any new stress and we can paint anything we want on our 'life canvas' especially in those first few moments. Why not be grateful? How about appreciating the present moment? Yes, right then, first thought after awakening:

I am grateful for _____.

These are some of my favorite words of gratitude and appreciation used first thing in the morning.

> *I am so grateful to be alive and breathing.*
> *Thank you for this beautiful life, Lord.*
> *I am blessed with the best most loving family, thank you.*
> *I so appreciate this safe, warm, comfortable bed!*
> *Thank you for my healthy body, happy life and the best friends that life could offer.*

Gratitude is a choice. Happiness is a choice. If you start your day with a few minutes of grateful thoughts, words and feelings, you are pointed UP, my friend! Onward and upward. If you start your day with, "Oh God, another crappy day. I am exhausted. I don't feel good. I got up on the wrong side of the bed..." what direction are you pointing with that attitude? What direction will your life most likely take if you are aiming your mindset in that direction of dread, stress, and defeatism? It makes logical sense that if you plant seeds of doubt, fear and despondency that you will receive more of that in your life, right? So, if you go in the other direction and plant seeds of optimism, hope, goodness and thankfulness, what can you expect then? That's right, GREAT Things. Divine Blessings. Maybe even Miracles!

Let's discuss a very important word to this whole process that I used above: *Feelings.* Feelings and emotions are the engines behind our thoughts, ideas and beliefs. How strongly we *feel* will play a large part in how much power our Gratitude Practice will help us. If we just go through the motions and say some words while actually thinking and feeling about the weather, your— to-do-list, what someone said or did, what you are going to eat for breakfast, etc. you can't really expect this process to really help you feel better. It takes just a few minutes of focus. Why not give it your all? You will get out of it exactly what you put into it, just like everything else in life! More on Emotions later on...

Eating and Drinking

Without sustenance, we can only stay alive for days or weeks. When drinking your morning coffee, your fresh water throughout the day, or right before or during any of your meals, you should practice your 'gratitude muscle'. It really only takes a few seconds, but it can do so much for you and your body right before a meal. Your food will taste better, your body will relax and you will absorb and metabolize your food more efficiently. I usually say just one line, something such as, "Lord, I am grateful for this delicious, healthy food," even if it's a cheeseburger or a slice of pizza, because I know how powerful the intention is of Gratitude. True thankfulness can affect any situation, at any time. When cooking, I am always grateful for the smells, the colors, the textures, the thought of supplying my family with an abundant bounty of delicious healthy foods (even if I am cooking grilled cheese sandwiches!). There is power in intention and there is divinity in Gratitude.

Be sure to remember your practice when eating and drinking throughout the day. Sometimes it's our only practice and we don't remember to do it any other time, but if we remember our gratefulness related to food the seeds are planted from our first meal to our last and all of our drinks in between. It can also be a way not to drink too much alcohol, or anything else we may be letting go of, or being conscious of in our lives. When I am grateful for a delicious Cabernet and I am present to each sip, how it tastes, I only want one glass, or maybe even a few sips and I am satiated.

The Breath

This practice is as simple as they come, but as far from easy. We are all breathing, all the time. Sure, we could hold our breath for a few seconds or maybe even a couple of minutes, but after several minutes, life for the body would cease. The Breath sounds pretty important in that context does it not?

However, we rarely think about it, we take the breath for granted, we take the life giving experience as a given since it's been there as long as we can remember. When we put our attention on the breath, when we allow ourselves to relax, be and become grateful for each in and out breath, we are honoring it. By doing this practice whether we are sitting in meditation, during yoga, or just driving to work or doing chores, we are inviting in a very beautiful act of creation. Focusing on the breath, watching it flow into and out of our bodies, not changing our breathing pattern but simply watching the process, feeling it and becoming grateful for the life giving function, something very wonderful and powerful can be awakened within us.

To discuss this more deeply, I plan to write a completely separate book! For the time being, even if you have never meditated or done yoga, do not despair, this simple easy, gentle practice of watching the breath flow into and out of the body like waves moving on to a seashore can be more than enough to experience for a lifetime if we are able to deeply connect with the practice.

I often slowly repeat the words, "Thank you, Lord," or just, "Thank you," quietly or silently to myself as I relax enough to let the chatter in my mind fall away. This mantra brings the practice to a very co-creative divinely connected space that I thoroughly enjoy. Try out different ways to do this practice and see what works best for you.

The Senses

Sense of Sight:
Spending time truly seeing and not just taking our eyesight for granted can be a very revolutionizing experience. Not just what's straight ahead but your peripheral vision with a relaxed gaze focused on the colors, shapes, play of shadow and light. Imagine for a moment you are an artist painting on the canvas of your life. Do you see nature, beauty, love, pain or suffering? It can be anything at all, but the aim of this exercise is to simply see deeper than we ever have before.

Sense of Hearing:
Sound is vibration. See if you can really listen to sounds far away, close to you, even your own breath and heartbeat. Can you hear birds, cars, wind, a child's laugh? Listen to your favorite music like it's the first time you have ever heard it. Listen to your favorite person's voice, hear the vibration in their

throat, not just the words they say.

Sense of Taste:
Yum! Do you love the taste of food? God knows I do. I am a sweet and savory lover, some spice like curry and jalapenos. I can really enjoy food that is very alive with flavor and sometimes just food that is very fresh, just picked, etc. You can taste the life in it. What does your life taste like today?

Sense of Smell:
Ah, the aroma of life. Life always has a type of smell associated with it, right? It's always changing but it can be subtle and often very powerful, beautiful nostalgia, bringing us back to our Grandmother's kitchen, or a time when we were happy or scared. Our sense of smell is closely connected to brain function, memories and mood.

Sense of Touch:
What would we do without it? All of our senses are important, but we know what happens to people who go without a significant amount of human touch. We wither, we become sad, depressed and sick. However, there are many more wondrous opportunities with our sense of touch: water, wind, warm sun on our skin. Think for a moment on what your life would be like without the sense of touch.

What would our lives be without any of our senses? Makes sense (forgive the pun!) to take some time and consciously experience them, getting to know them on a deeper level, which will only create more opportunities to experience life fully.

Driving, Moving from Place to Place

We are moving beings, we are always on the move, whether traveling, going to work, going to meetings, running errands, picking up the kids (or the parents) or whatever. Fact is, we move. Whether just within our homes or outside of them, we rarely stay in bed all day and I do NOT recommend it if it can be avoided.

Guess what? We can be grateful as we do ALL of it. Remember, Gratitude is a choice. We can set an intention: today, every time I drive, the first thing I am going to do once I get in the car, before it's even moving, is to be grateful that I have a car, be grateful that it runs well, etc.

We can do the same thing when picking up the kids, we can be grateful that we were blessed with children or, if picking up a parent, that we still have a parent in our lives. Truth is, it's really not about the specifics, it's much more about the *intention* and the *feeling* we get when we feel appreciative and thankful. This feeling can really help move us where we want our mood, our attitude, even our presence, if the gratitude goes deep enough.

The Wild and Wonderful World of Emotions

Our emotional life is very powerful. In fact, in a way it *is* our life. We define and measure our lives by how we feel. We could have fifty million in the bank but have no friends or family and still feel absolutely terrible, or we could have the best family and friends in the world but feel terrible because we don't have enough money.

The situation isn't really what matters, it's how we meet our lives that does. If we meet our lives by intending to be grateful, thankful, loving, kind, generous, etc. the world will be much kinder to us. In other words, our emotions will be more what we hope to feel in our lives. We don't need to be a behavioral scientist or therapist to work with our emotions, we simply have to have a willingness to get to know ourselves better, to become aware of and put into practice what helps us live a better life. Gratitude can and will do that for you if you put it into action.

It has completely changed my whole emotional life. In my twenties, when I started this practice, I was AMAZED at how different I could feel after just a few short minutes of a simple Gratitude practice. At first, I thought I was kidding myself, or lying to myself. I had to let that conflict go and just allow myself to feel good. I learned to do it when all else around me was not looking so great. I learned that we can live life from the eye of the storm, if we choose to do so. Sure, it takes practice, but it is possible. We can do it, many people have.

We can approach and experience life with a Grateful Heart. Our heart is where our true spiritual and emotional life resides. Focus on your heart as you are reading this, gently, lovingly, put your attention there and simply become aware of what you feel, without judgement, criticism or trying to change anything. Just be with yourself for a few moments. Feel free to put the book down and simply feel your emotions.

Now, from that place of awareness, picture the person you love most in the world, alive or dead, in your life currently or not and just picture their happy smiling face and feel your love for them, your gratitude for them, your appreciation for them and the gift they have been in your life. You can do this with anyone you care about, appreciate, want to connect with, want to forgive, attract, etc.

See how you feel when you do this exercise, become an observer of your emotions. If you learn how to let your emotions flow, you can also learn to manage them, which in turn can help you manage your life, all with the simple practice of Gratitude.

The Gift of Nature

The gift of nature is one that I have sought refuge in thousands of times. As a young boy growing up near the water, I would ride my bike from my house for about a mile in my desire to be near the bay, close to the water. It was all consuming and as soon as I saw it, a feeling of total peace would envelop me.

At times, I couldn't get to the water but just finding a field and running, slow at first but then as fast as I could for as long as I could, was just as fulfilling. Breathing in the fresh air, seeing the beautiful sky, the smell of the fresh cut grass, would awaken something deep inside and remind me of what it was to be alive, to feel fulfilled, to experience life from an awakened, vibrant, vital place.

I still do this today, although I run much less frequently. These days I find great solace in my daily nature walks, sometimes since I only have ten or twenty minutes spare, it tends to be just around the block. A few times a week, I am blessed to do this practice of appreciating nature with my two-year-old son, watching him, appreciating him, thanking God for him, smelling the ocean air.

The energy I immediately tap into during this practice, I find truly divine. There is not much I enjoy more than when I am with those I love most, or simply by myself and focused on my inner being while *being* outside in nature, on a hike, at the beach, swimming in a lake, sailing on a boat.

Once again, all the practices listed here can be done while you are doing anything else in life. That is what makes a gratitude practice so wonderful, that you can do it anywhere, anytime, with anyone while enjoying the best life has to offer which, more often than not for me, is also the simplest, the slowest, the quietest times that life offers.

If it does not happen on its own; I choose to create time for it and to commit to my time in nature. Give nature a chance, see if you can work thirty minutes into your week, and then if you really enjoy it, you can end up making it a priority for your day every day, like it is for me. Who knows? Maybe I'll see you at the beach, at the park, at the lake....

Animals

Animals are a part of nature, however, I wanted to highlight them here because they have been very instrumental in my life at different points and I think can have a great effect on our lives, especially when done with significant consciousness. Just to be clear, what I am NOT talking about here is running out and buying a dog, cat or any other animal without seriously considering the responsibilities—the care, the time, the money, etc. that is involved in purchasing a pet.

In fact, there is no need whatsoever to purchase a pet to do this type of inner work. We can simply look at the birds outside our windows or get into nature and see what we see, or go to a zoo, a pet store or an animal shelter. We can also offer to care for our family's or friends' animal, take them for a walk, bring them a gift and invest some quality time with the animals that are available to you. Once you do find the correct way for you to be near animals that feel best to you, you can perform this simple practice at any time you are with them.

Do the Sense Exercise from earlier on in this chapter, to awaken your mind and body, and however you interact with them, simply *be* with your surroundings, the animals, nature as a whole. Notice how you feel, what comes up, thoughts and so on. Simply *being,* with no goals, no expectations, no changing it to be better, or more fun, etc. This practice is just about learning how "to be" as Shakespeare advises us. Animals are always being; they do not have egos like us, they are much more natural and simply act the way they are all the time.

We, on the other hand, hem and haw, feel fear, worry, stress, etc. We can learn from these animals how powerful it can be in our lives to have the skill of merely *being.* After doing this practice for a few minutes or longer, if it feels good, helpful or illuminating, notice at this point what you are feeling grateful for. You may find that you have some very different ideas, or inspirations after this practice. Follow the practice, see where it leads you and allow your inner guidance to be in the driver seat.

During Exercise

First of all, are you exercising for twenty minutes at least three or four times a week? That is the absolute minimum that a person from their teens to their seventies should be exercising in order to remain healthy. While you are exercising, whether you are walking, jogging, doing yoga, cross-fit, tai chi, qi gong, at the gym, etc. it's an amazing opportunity to be grateful for your life, for your body, your breath, your health, your working joints, your senses, for fresh air, the views that you can see while walking at the beach or through the woods or elsewhere. Your body will naturally be releasing feel-good endorphins, and if you start thinking and feeling good thoughts and emotions, you will really be lifted up.

Just think about what is called *runners' high*. If you have not experienced it, I recommend it very highly. When you combine it with a deep sense of gratitude and appreciation for what is your life, you are creating a very special space for a high-level experience. It's truly a reverent space, where I have felt aligned, in the zone, like I was invincible, unstoppable, maybe even immortal! So, hopefully you will take my advice and get out there, exercise, and allow yourself to feel great.

Evening

The evening is a really wonderful time to slow down and ease into your restful time before sleep. It's important to remember that whatever we bring with us in our minds and in our hearts to sleep with us will remain with us while we sleep. Especially after a gratitude-filled day, I love to simply look back and bask in the beauty of the day, remembering all the good things that have happened, all the blessings received. Another day of health, happiness, and prosperity, another day of peace, love and connection. I see my family's smiling faces, my clients' appreciative words, and all the other freedoms, gifts and joys that were present that day. Sometimes, even if I have had a 'tough' day, I focus on the simple blessings, the breath, the senses, moments of neutrality, whatever I can salvage as 'goodness' from the day.

Any Area of Your Life

So, I have laid out ten areas of my life that I picked based on the level of my enjoyment with the practice, as well as areas that I think will provide you, the reader, with a quality experience in your own practice. Now, it's time for you to get creative! Use the areas above that I recommend—which are great for me but which may not be great for you—keep pushing forward. It's important not to be too stuck in our ways.

You will enjoy your practice much more if you are instrumental in coming up with your own ideas and exploring what works best for your life, for your happiness, for your soul. Simply think about the things that you do on a daily and weekly basis. What would be a good fit to add a gratitude practice to? What is already fun that you do? Dance, music, cooking, making love, your work, talking to your favorite people? Remember, this is *your* practice, you can do whatever you want and you don't need me or anyone else telling you exactly what to do.

Teachers, like myself, are here to point towards what has worked best for ourselves and our students, but that does not mean you cannot come up with better ideas that really explode your joy and happiness in every direction.

It's very important to remember that we are divine, eternal beings. If you vibrate that, if you feel that in your heart, soul and being, nothing is impossible and if you combine a very powerful feeling place like that with a grateful, kind, compassionate, loving, and appreciative heart, the world will be yours.

There will be nothing you can't do, be or have. It's ALL up to you. What do you really, really, REALLY want?

You create your own life by what you think, feel, say and do. If you change that for the better, all you have ever dreamed of and wished for will be yours, at the very least on its way to you. If you are doing all this work while feeling grateful and appreciative, your life will always be overall pretty darn happy and joyful. Why not, right? And why not *you*, right?! You deserve it, and you are worthy of experiencing all the joy, as a divine child of The Universe that you can invite into your life.

"Gratitude makes sense of our past, brings peace for today, and creates a vision for tomorrow."

--Melody Beattie

Information About
Matt O'Grady Coaching

Individual, Group and Workshop Options available.

For more details email:
team@mattogradycoaching.com

Want Matt O'Grady to speak at your next event? In person and virtual options available.

To be added to Matt's weekly email list go here: http://eepurl.com/byNz39